The Essentials of Academic Writing for International Students

Most international students need to write essays and reports for exams and coursework, but writing good academic English is one of the most demanding tasks students face. *The Essentials of Academic Writing for International Students* has been developed to help these students succeed in their assignments – quickly!

This course has a clear, easy-to-follow structure. In the first part, Process and Skills, each stage of the writing process is demonstrated and practised, from selecting suitable sources, reading, note-making and planning through to rewriting and proofreading.

Each unit contains examples, explanations and exercises, for use in the classroom or for self-study. The units are clearly organised to allow teachers and students find the help they need with writing tasks.

The second part of the book, Elements of Writing, deals with key areas for improving accuracy, such as academic vocabulary, using numbers and punctuation. This section can be linked with the first part or used for reference or self-study.

All international students wanting to maximise their academic potential will find this practical and easy-to-use book an invaluable guide to writing in English for their degree courses.

- All elements of writing are clearly explained
- Full range of practice exercises, with answer key included
- Use of authentic academic texts and examples
- Fully up to date, with sections on finding electronic sources and evaluating internet material

Stephen Bailey is a freelance writer of materials for English for Academic Purposes. He has taught students in Barcelona, Tokyo, Johor Bahru and Prague, and more recently at Derby University and the University of Nottingham. His other books include *Academic Writing: A Handbook for International Students* and *Academic Writing for International Students of Business* (Routledge).

The Essentials of Academic Writing for International Students

Stephen Bailey

Routledge
Taylor & Francis Group

LONDON AND NEW YORK

First published 2015
by Routledge
2 Park Square, Milton Park, Abingdon, Oxon OX14 4RN

and by Routledge
711 Third Avenue, New York, NY 10017

*Routledge is an imprint of the Taylor & Francis Group,
an informa business*

British Library Cataloguing in Publication Data
A catalogue record for this book is available from the
British Library

Library of Congress Cataloging in Publication Data
Bailey, Stephen, 1947– author.
The essentials of academic writing for international
students/Stephen Bailey.
pages cm
Includes bibliographical references and index.
1. Academic writing. 2. English language –Textbooks for
foreign speakers. 3. English language – Rhetoric. I. Title.
P301.5.A27B35 2015
808′.0428 – dc23
2014049456

ISBN: 978-1-138-88561-5 (hbk)
ISBN: 978-1-138-88562-2 (pbk)
ISBN: 978-1-315-71534-6 (ebk)

Typeset in Galliard
by Florence Production Ltd, Stoodleigh, Devon, UK
Printed by Bell and Bain Ltd, Glasgow

Contents

Acknowledgements

I would like to thank all the colleagues I have worked with over the years, in a number of different countries, who have shared their ideas and enthusiasm with me. Their support and interest has been vital in developing these materials. Above all, my wife Rene has contributed in many ways to the success of this project, in particular by her knowledge of, and interest in, the finer points of English language.

Introduction

The Essentials of Academic Writing has been developed to help international students with their written assignments in English-medium colleges and universities. This course is designed to explain and practise the skills involved in essay and report writing, and can be used at undergraduate and postgraduate levels. It is suitable for both subject-specific (e.g. Business, Law) and multidisciplinary courses in English for Academic Purposes (EAP). The inclusion of an answer key allows it to be used for both classroom teaching and self-study.

The course is based on extensive experience of preparing international students to write effectively in English. It aims to address their most common difficulties directly, especially with regard to referencing, style, vocabulary and potential plagiarism. In addition, concerns about the selection and processing of suitable academic texts and the lack of critical thinking are fully addressed.

Clearly, teachers do not expect international students to write perfect English, and usually make allowance for them in marking their work. However, students should consider that their academic course gives them an ideal chance to strengthen their writing skills, not only for academic success, but also in preparation for their future career. Most large companies and organisations now expect their employees to communicate in written English, and this book provides an opportunity to develop this ability.

Structure

Part 1, **Process and Skills**, is a step-by-step guide in 12 units to the complete process of academic writing, from finding suitable sources and improving reading methods to rewriting and proofreading. Each stage of the process is linked to a key writing skill, so that in Unit 1.7, for instance, summarising and paraphrasing are linked with an understanding of the use of synonyms. Each unit contains a range of practice exercises and concludes with a progress check. The focus throughout is on clear, simple explanation and maximum student involvement.

Part 2, **Elements of Writing**, consists of 10 units that cover the most important issues of accuracy for student writers, such as vocabulary, making comparisons and using numbers. These units are arranged alphabetically and can be studied as supplementary material for Part 1, or, alternatively, they can be used for self-study and reference.

The two units in **Part 3**, **Writing Models**, give examples of reports and a longer essay. These are followed by a final progress test, the answer key and an index. As far as possible, the texts and essay titles are authentic examples taken from a range of disciplines. Both teachers and students should find that this book is easy to use and contains the ingredients for achieving success in written assignments.

Using the book

Instructions are printed as shown here:

■ Discuss with a partner

Answers are provided for most exercises in the answer key at the end of the book. If no definite answer can be given, an example answer is usually provided.

The **index** on page 229 can be used to locate specific information.

While every effort has been made to make the book both accurate and relevant, improvements can always be introduced, and I would be glad to receive any comments or suggestions for future editions from teachers and students.

Stephen Bailey
stephen.bailey@w3z.co.uk

How Much Do You Know about Academic Writing?

Try these 20 questions to find out!

1   Is there a difference between an essay and a report?

2   What kind of words are 'because', 'however' and 'since' examples of?

3   What is the name of this punctuation mark (')?

4   Give three situations where capital letters should be used.

5   What is 'bias' in written work?

6   A paragraph is a group of sentences dealing with one topic. True or false?

7   Give one reason for using quotations in an essay.

8   Which of these words are suitable for academic use: child/woman/ guy/kid/girl?

9   Give two situations where these marks are used in written work (' ')?

10   What is the difference between proofreading and rewriting?

11   'Unkind', 'revisit' and 'subway' all contain examples of what?

12   Give an example of an abbreviation commonly used in academic writing.

13   Where would you find an abstract in an academic article? What is its purpose?

14   Give one reason for providing references in academic work.

15   Find a synonym for 'country'.

16   What is the difference between paraphrasing and summarising?

17   What is the name for the section of an essay between the introduction and the conclusion?

18   'Research', 'progress' and 'knowledge' are all nouns. What kind of noun?

19   What is the difference between a flow chart and a pie chart?

20   Give two reasons for using brackets ( ) in written work.

Answers on p. 187

Process and Skills

Introduction to Writing

Most academic courses test students through written assignments. These tasks include coursework, which may take weeks to write, and exam answers, which often have to be completed in an hour. This unit explains:

- the names of different writing tasks
- the format of long and short writing tasks
- the main features of academic texts
- the use of paragraphs

1 Why do we write?

Academic writing allows us to share ideas, discoveries and arguments with other students and researchers in our field, all over the world. Our purpose may be:

- to report on a piece of research the writer has conducted
- to discuss a subject of common interest and give the writer's view
- to synthesise research done by others on a topic

■ Can you suggest any other reasons?

- _____
- _____

Whatever the purpose, it is useful to think about the probable readers of your work: you need to explain your ideas to them as clearly as possible. This is why academic writing is different from the style of newspapers or novels. For example, it is generally agreed that academic writing attempts to be accurate. What are its other features?

■ **Working alone or in a group, list your ideas below.**

● _____

● _____

2 Types of academic writing

Below are the most common types of written work produced by students.

■ **Match the terms on the left to the definitions on the right.**

Notes	A piece of research, either individual or group work, with the topic chosen by the student(s).
Report	The longest piece of writing normally done by a student (20,000+ words) often for a higher degree, on a topic chosen by the student.
Project	A written record of the main points of a text or lecture, for a student's personal use.
Essay	A general term for any academic essay, report, presentation or article.
Dissertation/Thesis	A description of something a student has done (e.g. conducting a survey or experiment).
Paper	The most common type of written work, with the title given by the teacher, normally 1,000–5,000 words.

3 The format of long and short writing tasks

The layout of academic work varies from subject to subject, but the following formats are widely used. Short essays (including exam answers) generally have this pattern:

Introduction

Main body

Conclusion

Longer essays and reports may include:

Introduction

Main body

    Literature review

    Case study

    Discussion

Conclusion

References

Appendices

Dissertations and journal articles may have:

Abstract

List of contents

List of tables

Introduction

Main body

    Literature review

    Case study

    Findings

    Discussion

Conclusion

Acknowledgements

References

Appendices

■ **Find the words in the lists above that match the following definitions.**

a)   A short summary that explains the paper's purpose and main findings.

b)   A list of all the sources the writer has mentioned in the text.

_____

c)   A section at the end where additional information is included.

_____

d)   A short section where people who have helped the writer are thanked.

_____

e)   Part of the main body in which the work of other writers on the topic is discussed.

_____

f)   A section where one particular example is described in detail.

_____

4 The components of academic writing

■ Read the essay introduction below. Underline and label (a–f) examples of components from the box.

a) sentence	b) heading	c) subtitle
d) paragraph	e) title	f) phrase

A fishy story

Misleading health claims regarding omega-3 fatty acids

Introduction

There has been considerable discussion recently about the benefits of omega-3 fatty acids in the diet. It is claimed that these reduce the risk of cardiovascular disease and may even combat obesity. Consequently food producers have added omega-3s to products ranging from margarine to soft drinks in an attempt to make their products appear healthier and hence increase sales.

However, consumers may be unaware that there are two types of omega-3s. The best (long-chain fatty acids) are derived from fish, but others (short-chain fatty acids) come from cheaper sources such as soya. This latter group have not been shown to produce the health benefits linked to the long-chain variety. According to Tamura *et al.* (2009) positive results may only be obtained either by eating oily fish three times a week, or by taking daily supplements containing 500 mg of eicosapentaenoic acid (EPA) or docosahexaenoic acid (DHA).

5 Other common text features

a) **Reference** to sources using **citation**: *According to Tamura et al. (2009)*

b) The use of **abbreviations** to save space: *docosahexaenoic acid (DHA)*

c) **Italics**: used to show words from other languages: Tamura *et al.* (= and others)

d) **Brackets**: used to give extra information or to clarify a point: ... *but others (short-chain fatty acids) come from cheaper sources such as soya.*

6 Writing in paragraphs

■ Discuss the following questions:

What is the purpose of paragraphs?

Why are texts divided into paragraphs?

How long are paragraphs?

■ Read the text below and divide it into a suitable number of paragraphs.

Investment strategies

Most people want to invest for the future, to cover unexpected financial difficulties and provide security. Different people, however, tend to have different requirements, so that a 25-year-old just leaving university would be investing for long-term capital growth, whereas a 60-year-old who had just retired would probably invest for income. Despite these differences, certain principles apply in most cases. The first issue to consider is risk. In general, the greater the degree of risk, the higher the return. Shares, for example, which can quickly rise or fall in value, typically have a higher yield than bonds, which offer greater stability. Therefore all investors must decide how much risk is appropriate in their particular situation. Diversification must also be considered in an investment strategy. Wise investors usually seek to spread their investments across a variety of geographical and business sectors. As accurate predictions of the future are almost impossible, it is best to have as many options as possible. A further consideration is investor involvement. Some investors choose a high degree of involvement and want to buy and sell regularly, constantly watching the markets. But personal involvement can be time-consuming and worrying, and many prefer to leave the management of their portfolios to professional fund managers.

7 Progress check

■   Revise some of the vocabulary (all nouns) used in this unit by matching the words on the left with the meanings on the right.

acknowledgement	a group of words commonly used together
appendix	a part of a complete thing
assignment	lettering angled to the right
citation	a lengthy piece of work written for a higher degree
component	additional information added to the end of a paper
dissertation	a piece of work on a topic chosen by the student
format	any task given to students by their teacher
italics	**recognition of assistance given to a writer**
phrase	a link, included in the text, to a reference
project	the organisation or layout of a text

UNIT 1.2 Reading

Assessing Sources/Using Prefixes and Suffixes

Preparing to write generally involves extensive reading. Although students often underestimate the importance of reading, on any course it is vital to be able to find and understand the most relevant and suitable sources quickly. This unit:

- examines the most appropriate text types for academic use
- explores ways of locating relevant material in the library
- explains how understanding prefixes and suffixes can help build vocabulary

PROCESS: ASSESSING SOURCES

1 Types of text

■ The table below lists the most common written sources used by students. Work with a partner and discuss their likely advantages and disadvantages. Complete the table.

Text type	Advantages	Disadvantages
Textbook	*Written for students*	*May be too general or outdated*
Website		
Journal article		
Official report (e.g. from government)		
Newspaper or magazine article		
E-book		

2 Finding suitable texts

You may need to read a variety of types of texts, such as websites or journal articles, for your course. It is important to identify the most suitable texts by recognising their features, which will help you to assess their value.

■ **You are studying Tourism Marketing. Read the text extracts 2.1–2.3 below and decide which are the most suitable for academic use. Complete the table below with reasons.**

Text	Suitable?
2.1	
2.2	
2.3	

2.1

To promote tourism and market destination, it is important to study the tourists' attitude, behaviour and demand. The studies of Levitt (1986) and Kotler and Armstrong (1994) suggest that an understanding of consumer behaviour may help with the marketing planning process in tourism marketing. The research of consumer behaviour is the key to the underpinning of all marketing activity which is carried out to develop, promote and sell tourism products (Swarbrooke and Horner, 1999; Asad, 2005). Therefore, the study of consumer behaviour has become necessary for the sake of tourism marketing.

2.2

The romance of travel has always fascinated me, and our recent trip to Thailand lived up to expectations. We flew from Dubai and after a comfortable flight arrived in Bangkok just as the sun was rising. Our stay in the city lasted only a couple of days before we set off for the hill country around Chang Mai, where we were planning to visit some of the indigenous tribes who live in this mountainous region. When we arrived the weather was rather disappointing, but after a day the heavy rain gave way to sparkling clear sunshine.

2.3

Holiday trips to the Antarctic have quadrupled in the past decade and last year more than 46,000 people visited the land mass and surrounding oceans. However, safety fears and concerns about the impact visitors are having on the delicate frozen landscape have soared and members of the Antarctic Treaty – an agreement between 28 nations, including the UK, on the use of the continent – are now meeting to discuss ways to regulate tourism.

British officials are seeking to establish a 'strategic agreement for tourism' around the South Pole. If successful, it will see treaty members introduce new measures to improve the safety of tourist trips, while also reducing the impact that visitors will have on the environment. The regulations could see limits on the number of ships and landings, restrictions on how close they come to shore, a ban on building tourist facilities and hotels on the continent, and rules on waste discharges from ships.

Extract 2.1 illustrates the main features of an academic text:

a)   An impersonal style: . . . *it is important to study tourists' attitude, behaviour and demand.*

b)   Use of references: *The studies of Levitt (1986) and Kotler and Armstrong (1994) . . .*

c)   Semi-formal vocabulary: . . . *an understanding of consumer behaviour may help with the marketing planning process in tourism marketing.*

3 Using reading lists

Your teacher may give you a printed reading list, or it may be available online through the library website. The list will usually include textbooks, journal articles and websites. If the list is electronic, there will be links to the library catalogue to let you check on the availability of the material. If the list is printed, you will have to use the library catalogue to find the texts. You do not have to read every word of a book because it is on the list. Your teacher will tell you which parts are the most important.

On reading lists, you will find the following formats:

Books   Miles, T. R. *Dyslexia: a hundred years on*/T.R. Miles and
                     Elaine Miles, 2nd ed. Open University Press, 1999.

Journal articles Paulesu E. *et al.* Dyslexia: cultural diversity and biological
                     unity. *Science*, 2001, 291, pages 2165–2167.

Websites   http://www.well.ox.ac.uk/monaco/dyslexia.shtml

4 Using library catalogues

University and college libraries usually have online catalogues. These allow students to search for the materials they want in various ways. If you know the title and author's name, it is easy to check if the book is available, but if you are making a search for material on a specific topic you may have to vary the search terms. For instance, if you have been given an essay title:

'Are there any practical advantages in constructing tall buildings? Illustrate your answer with reference to some recent skyscrapers.'

you might try: **Skyscrapers** or **Skyscraper construction** or **Design of tall buildings**.

If you use a very specific phrase, you will probably only find a few titles. 'Skyscraper construction', for example, only produced three items in one library catalogue, but a more general term such as 'skyscrapers' found 57.

■ You have entered the term 'skyscrapers' in the library catalogue, and these are the first six results. In order to answer the essay title above, which would you select to borrow? Give your reasons.

Full details	Title	Year	Location	Holdings
<u>1</u>	Skyscrapers : a history of the world's most extraordinary buildings/by Judith Dupré; introductory interview with Adrian Smith	2013	Main library	<u>Availability</u>
<u>2</u>	Manhattan skyscrapers/Eric P. Nash; photographs by Norman McGrath. 3rd ed.	2010	Main library	<u>Availability</u>
<u>3</u>	Art deco San Francisco [electronic resource] : the architecture of Timothy Pflueger/Therese Poletti ; photography by Tom Paiva.	2008	Fine Arts library	<u>Availability</u>
<u>4</u>	A cost-effective analysis of skyscraper development/James Moncur.	2008	Main library	<u>Availability</u>
<u>5</u>	Tall buildings: image of the skyscraper/Scott Johnson.	2008	Fine Arts library	<u>Availability</u>
<u>6</u>	Skyscrapers: a social history of the very tall building in America/by George H. Douglas.	2004	Main library	<u>Availability</u>

Full details

If you click on this, you will get more information about the book, including the number of pages and a summary of the contents. If a book has had more than one edition, it suggests that it is a successful title.

Year

The books are listed by the most recent first; always try to use the most up-to-date sources.

Location

Many large universities have more than one library. This tells you which one the book is kept in.

Holdings

If you click on availability, it will tell you how many copies the library holds and if they are available to borrow or out on loan.

SKILLS: USING PREFIXES AND SUFFIXES

5 How prefixes and suffixes work

Reading academic texts quickly and accurately involves developing a wide vocabulary. Looking up new words can be time-consuming, but understanding the meaning of prefixes and suffixes can help you work out the meaning of a word. Prefixes and suffixes are the first and last parts of certain words:

Prefixes change or give the meaning.

Suffixes show the meaning or the word class (e.g. noun, verb).

'Unsustainable' is an example of a word containing a prefix and suffix. Words like this are much easier to understand if you know how prefixes and suffixes affect word meaning.

Prefix	Meaning	STEM	Meaning	Suffix	Word class/ Meaning
un-	negative	**sustain**	support	**-able**	adjective/ ability

The rate of growth was unsustainable (i.e. could not be continued).

6 Prefixes

a) Negative prefixes: NON-, UN-, IN-, IM-, MIS-, DE- and DIS- often give adjectives and verbs a negative meaning: **non**sense, **un**clear, **in**capable, **im**possible, **mis**hear, **de**crease, **dis**agree.

b) A number of prefixes define meaning (e.g. PRE- usually means 'before', hence **pre**fer, **pre**history and, of course, **pre**fix!)

■ Find the meaning(s) of each prefix (NB: some prefixes have more than one meaning).

Common prefixes of meaning

Prefix	Example	Example sentence	Meaning
anti	antidepressant	*Antidepressant drugs are often overprescribed.*	*against*
auto	automatically	*Over-18s automatically have the right to vote.*	
co	coordinator	*The coordinator invited them to a meeting.*	
ex	ex-president	*The ex-president gave a speech on climate change.*	
ex	exclusive	*It is difficult to join such an exclusive club.*	
fore	forecast	*The long-term forecast is for higher inflation.*	
inter	intervention	*Early medical intervention saves lives.*	
macro	macroeconomics	*Keynes focused on macroeconomics.*	
micro	microscope	*She examined the tiny animals with a microscope.*	
multi	multinational	*Ford is a multinational motor company.*	
over	oversleep	*He missed the lecture as he overslept.*	
poly	polyglot	*She was a true polyglot, speaking five languages.*	
post	postpone	*The meeting is postponed until next Monday.*	
re	retrain	*The film retrained staff to use the new software.*	
sub	subtitle	*Chinese films often have subtitles in the West.*	
trans	transmitter	*Early radio transmitters were short-range.*	
under	undergraduate	*Most undergraduate courses last three years.*	
under	undercook	*Eating undercooked meat can be dangerous.*	

7 Practice A

Prefixes allow new words to be created (e.g. 'unfriend' – to delete a 'friend' from social media).

■ **Suggest possible meanings for the recently developed words in bold.**

a)   Students often **underestimate** the importance of reading.

b)   They found that the plane was **overbooked** and had to wait for the next flight.

c)   The **microclimate** in this district allows early vegetables to be grown.

d)   It is claimed that computers have created a **post-industrial** economy.

e)   The students were **underwhelmed** by the quality of the lecture.

8 Suffixes

Some suffixes such as -ION, -IVE or -LY help the reader find the word class (e.g. noun, verb or adjective).

Word class suffixes

Nouns	-ER often indicates a person: *teacher, gardener*
	-EE can show a person who is the subject: *employee, trainee*
	-ISM and -IST are often used with belief systems and their supporters: *socialism/socialist*
	-NESS converts an adjective into a noun: *sad/sadness*
	-ION changes a verb to a noun: *convert/conversion*
Adjectives	-IVE *effective, constructive*
	-AL *commercial, agricultural*
	-IOUS *precious, serious*
Verbs	-ISE/-IZE to form verbs from adjectives: *private/privatise*
	NB: In the US, only -IZE spelling is used, but both forms are accepted in the UK
Adverbs	-LY most (but not all) adverbs have this suffix: *happily, finally*

Meaning suffixes

A few suffixes contribute to the meaning of the word:

-ABLE has the meaning of 'ability': *a **watchable** film,* **changeable** *weather*

-WARDS means 'in the direction of': *the ship sailed **northwards***

-FUL and –LESS: *hopeful news, a **leaderless** team*

9 Practice B

■ Study each sentence and find the meaning of the words underlined.

a) The film is an Anglo-Italian <u>co-production</u> made by a <u>subsidiary</u> company.

b) When the car crashed, she screamed <u>involuntarily</u> but was <u>unharmed</u>.

c) Using <u>rechargeable</u> batteries has <u>undoubted</u> benefits for the environment.

d) The <u>unavailability</u> of the product is due to the <u>exceptional</u> weather.

e) The <u>miscommunication</u> led to a <u>reorganisation</u> of their software system.

10 Progress check

■ You are preparing to write an essay on 'Future telecommunication systems'. Read the text below and discuss with a partner whether it is suitable to use in your work.

ZEPHYR

Satellites in earth orbit are vital for modern telecommunication systems, but launching satellites is costly. A possible <u>inexpensive</u> alternative is currently being trialled by Airbus, a large airplane manufacturer. This is an <u>unmanned</u>, <u>ultralight</u> aircraft with a 23-metre <u>wingspan</u> which can stay in the air for months. During daylight hours it flies, using solar power, at high altitude, while at night it flies lower, using its <u>rechargeable</u> lithium-sulphur batteries. In order to reduce weight the plane has no <u>undercarriage</u>, but as its speed is only 22 kph this is <u>inessential</u>.

The aircraft has been named Zephyr and is designed for use in <u>subequatorial</u> zones where there is always enough daylight to recharge the batteries. In these areas these planes could act as relays for phone calls and internet communication, avoiding the need for ground-based <u>infrastructure</u>. When testing is completed and Zephyr becomes available commercially it should provide a low-cost alternative to satellite technology.

Source: Technology Today, September 2012, p.56

■ List the words underlined. Find their word class and possible meanings.

Reading
Critical Approaches/
Argument and Discussion

Students are expected to take a critical approach to sources, and this requires a good understanding of written texts. This unit:

- explains effective reading methods
- examines common text features, including abstracts
- explores and practises critical analysis of texts
- demonstrates ways of showing understanding of both sides of an argument
- shows how to present your findings in a suitable academic manner

PROCESS: CRITICAL APPROACHES

1 Reading methods

International students often find that reading academic texts in the quantity required for their courses is a demanding task. Yet students will not benefit from attending lectures and seminars unless the preparatory reading is done promptly, while most writing tasks require extensive reading.

Moreover, academic texts often contain new vocabulary and phrases, and may be written in a rather formal style. This means that special methods have to be learnt to cope with the volume of reading required. Clearly, you do not have time to read every word published on the topic you are studying, so you must first choose carefully what you read and then assess it thoroughly. The chart on p. 20 illustrates the best approach to choosing suitable texts.

■ Complete the empty boxes in the chart with the following techniques:

- Read intensively to make notes on key points
- Scan text for information you need (e.g. names)
- Survey text features (e.g. abstract, contents, index)

Choosing suitable texts

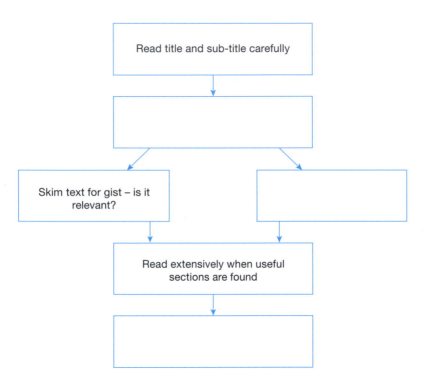

Read title and sub-title carefully

Skim text for gist – is it relevant?

Read extensively when useful sections are found

2 Titles, subtitles and text features

Many books and articles have both a title and subtitle:

> *The Right to Have Rights: Citizenship Practice and the Political Constitution of the EU*

The title is usually shorter and may aim to be eye-catching; the subtitle often gives more information about the focus. After finding a relevant title, it is worth checking the following text features before starting to read:

Author: Is the writer well known in his or her field? What else has he or she published?

Publication date and edition: Do not use a first edition if there is a (revised) second edition available.

Abstract: See section 3 below.

Contents: A list of the main chapters or sections. This should tell you how much space is given to the topic you are researching.

Introduction or preface: This is where the author often explains his or her reasons for writing, and also describes how the text is organised.

References: This list shows all the sources used by the author and referred to in the text (in the US, this is usually called a bibliography). It should give you some suggestions for further reading.

Index: An alphabetical list of all the topics and names mentioned in a book. If, for example, you are looking for information about a person, the index will tell you if that person is mentioned, and how often.

3 Reading abstracts

Abstracts are normally found in peer-reviewed journal articles, where they are a kind of summary to allow researchers to decide if it is worth reading the full article. As a student, you will not normally have to write abstracts, but it is important to be able to read them effectively.

■ Study this example:

Citizenship Norms and the Expansion of Political Participation

A growing chorus of scholars laments the decline of political participation in America, and the negative implications of this trend for American democracy. This article questions this position – arguing that previous studies misdiagnosed the sources of political change and the consequences of changing norms of citizenship for Americans' political engagement. Citizenship norms are shifting from a pattern of duty-based citizenship to engaged citizenship. Using data from the 2005 'Citizenship, Involvement, Democracy' survey of the Center for Democracy and Civil Society (CDACS) I describe these two faces of citizenship, and trace their impact on political participation. Rather than the erosion of participation, this norm shift is altering and expanding the patterns of political participation in America.

(Dalton, R.J. (2008) *Political Studies* 56 (1) pp. 76–98).

Abstracts normally have a standard structure:

a) Background   c) Method of research

b) Aim and thesis of paper   d) Results of research

■ Underline and label (a–d) these components in the abstract above.

4 Assessing internet sources critically

You cannot afford to waste time on texts that are unreliable or out of date. If you are using material that is not on the reading list, you must assess it critically to ensure that the material is trustworthy. Internet sources are plentiful and convenient, but you need to ask several questions about each website:

- Is this a reputable site, for example with .ac (= academic) in the URL?
- Is the name of the author given, and is he or she well known in the field?
- Is the language of the text in a suitable academic style?
- Are there any obvious errors in the text (e.g. spelling mistakes) that suggest a careless approach?

■ Compare these two internet texts on deforestation (the loss of forests). Which is likely to be more reliable?

4.1

We are destroying the last of our vital natural resources, just as we are starting to wake up to how precious they are. Rainforest once covered 14% of the land now it's down to a mere 6%. Scientists predict that the rest could disappear in less than 40 years. Thousands of acres are cut down each second with dire consequences for the countries involved and the planet as a whole. Scientists estimate that we loose 50,000 species every year, many species every second including 137 plant types (not even species but whole groups of plant species) and as these plants disappear before science can record them so does the chance to gain helpful knowledge and possible medicines.

4.2

The scale of human pressures on ecosystems everywhere has increased enormously in the last few decades. Since 1980 the global economy has tripled in size and the world's population has increased by 30%. Consumption of everything on the planet has risen - at a cost to our ecosystems. In 2001, The World Resources Institute estimated that the demand for rice, wheat, and corn is expected to grow by 40% by 2020, increasing irrigation water demands by 50% or more. They further reported that the demand for wood could double by the year 2050; unfortunately it is still the tropical forests that supply the bulk of the world's demand.

There are several aspects of 4.1 that should make the reader cautious: the style is very personal (we are . . .) and informal (it's down to . . .) and there is a word used wrongly ('loose' instead of 'lose'). No sources are provided. But even more disturbing is carelessness with facts. Is it really possible that thousands of acres of rainforest are being cut down *every second*? The writer also claims that many species are being lost *every second*, but if we take the figure of 50,000 per year it means one species is lost every 10 minutes. Clearly, the writer is seeking to dramatise the subject, but it is quite unsuitable as an academic source. In contrast, the second text is written in accurate, semi-formal language and includes a source. It seems likely to be more reliable.

5 Critical thinking

Even when you feel that a text is reliable and that you can safely use it as a source, it is still important to adopt a critical attitude towards it. This approach is perhaps easiest to learn when reading, but is important for all other academic work (i.e. listening, discussing and writing). Critical thinking means not just passively accepting what you hear or read, but instead actively questioning and assessing it. As you read, you should ask yourself the following questions:

a)   What are the key ideas in this?
b)   Does the argument of the writer develop logically, step by step?
c)   Are the examples given helpful? Would other examples be better?
d)   Does the author have any bias (leaning to one side or the other)?

e)   Does the evidence presented seem reliable, in my experience?

f)   Do I agree with the writer's views?

■ **Read critically the following two articles on universities.**

5.1 COLLEGE CONCERNS

Despite their dominance of global league tables (e.g. Shanghai Rankings Consultancy) American universities currently face significant criticism. The American Enterprise Institute (AEI) and the Goldwater Institute have recently published negative reports on US universities, while a highly critical book (Hacker and Dreifus) was published in 2010. The critics focus on the rising costs of American higher education, which have increased at a much faster rate than inflation, resulting in a situation where even middle-class families are finding the expense unsupportable.

Another target of criticism is the focus on research at the expense of teaching. Students rarely meet the 'star' professors, being taught instead by badly-paid graduate students. It is claimed that in one year nearly half of Harvard's history professors were on sabbatical leave. As a consequence, students work less; according to the AEI they currently study for 14 hours per week, whereas 50 years ago the figure was 24 hours per week. Despite this the proportion of students gaining a first or 2.1 degree has increased significantly: a situation described by the critics as 'grade inflation'.

5.2 A BRIGHTER TOMORROW?

There is little doubt that a university degree is the key to a better future for any student. Despite the costs involved in terms of fees, it has been calculated that the average UK university graduate will earn £400,000 ($600,000) more over his or her lifetime compared to a non-graduate. Possession of a degree should also assist a graduate find a satisfying job more quickly and give greater prospects for promotion inside the chosen career. A degree from a British university is recognised all over the world as proof of a high quality education.

A university course will not only provide students with up-to-date knowledge in their subject area, but also provide practice with the essential skills required by many employers today, such as the ability to communicate effectively using ICT, or the skills of team working and problem solving. In addition, living away from home in an international atmosphere gives the opportunity to make new friends from all over the world, and build networks of contacts that may be invaluable in a future career.

■ List any statements from the articles that you find unreliable, and add comments to explain your doubts in the table below. Then decide which article you find more reliable overall.

Statements	Comments
5.1	
5.2	

SKILLS: ARGUMENT AND DISCUSSION

6 Discussion vocabulary

Essay titles commonly ask students to 'discuss' a topic:

'Children will learn a foreign language more easily if it is integrated with another subject – discuss.'

This requires an evaluation of both the benefits and disadvantages of the topic, with a section of the essay, sometimes headed 'Discussion', in which a summary of these is made. The following vocabulary can be used:

+	−
benefit	drawback
advantage	disadvantage
a positive aspect	a negative feature
pro (informal)	con (informal)
plus (informal)	minus (informal)
one major advantage is . . .	a serious drawback is . . .

***One serious drawback** to integrating content and language is the demand it places on the teacher.*

■ Fill the gaps in the following paragraph using language from the table above.

Every year millions of students choose to study in a foreign country. This can have considerable a) _____ such as the chance to experience another culture, but also involves certain b) _____, which may include feelings of isolation or homesickness. Another c) _____ aspect may be the high cost, involving both fees and living expenses. However, most students appear to find that the d) _____ outweigh the e) _____, and that the chance to join an international group of students is a major f) _____ in developing a career.

7 The language of discussion

In discussion, avoid subjective language such as *in my opinion* or *personally, I think* . . .

Use impersonal phrases instead such as:

It is generally accepted that	working from home saves commuting time . . .
It is widely agreed that	email and the internet reduce reliance on an office . . .
Most people	appear to need face-to-face contact with colleagues . . .
It is probable that	more companies will encourage working from home . . .
The evidence suggests that	certain people are better at self-management . . .

When you are supporting your opinions with sources, use phrases such as:

According to Emerson (2003)	few companies have developed clear policies . . .
Poledna (2007) claims that	most employees benefit from flexible arrangements . . .

8 Organisation

The discussion can be organised in two ways: either by grouping the benefits in one section and the disadvantages in another (vertical), or by examining the subject from different viewpoints (horizontal). For example, the following essay title can be discussed in the two ways as shown:

'Prisons do little to reform criminals and their use should be limited – discuss.'

a) Vertical

Drawbacks
Prisons are expensive, may be 'universities of crime', most prisoners reoffend after leaving, many prisoners have mental health problems that are untreated.

Benefits
Prisons isolate dangerous criminals from society, act as a deterrent to criminal activity, may provide education or treatment (e.g. for drug addiction), provide punishment for wrongdoing.

Discussion
Numbers of prisoners are rising in many countries, which suggests that the system is failing. Evidence that short sentences are of little value. But prisons will always be necessary for some violent criminals, and as deterrent.

b) Horizontal

Economic
High costs of keeping prisoners secure. Compare with economics of other forms of punishment.

Ethical
Do prisons reform criminals? What rights should prisoners have? Cases of wrongful imprisonment.

Social
Effect on families of prisoners, especially female prisoners with children. But also necessary to consider the victims of crime, especially violent crime, and provide punishment for wrongdoing.

Discussion
Number of prisoners is rising in many countries, which suggests that the system is failing. Evidence that short sentences are of little value, while cost of prison system is rising. But prisons will always be necessary for some violent criminals, and as deterrent.

■ **What are the advantages of each format (i.e. vertical and horizontal)?**

9 Practice

You have to write an essay titled:

'Working from home can be positive for many companies and their employees – discuss.'

■ **Brainstorm the positive and negative aspects in the table below, and then write an outline using one of the structures (vertical or horizontal) above.**

+	−
No time wasted commuting to work	

10 Counterarguments

Counterarguments are ideas that are opposite to your views. In an academic discussion, you must show that you are familiar with both sides of the argument, and provide reasons to support your position. It is usual to deal with the counterarguments first, before giving your view.

■ **What is the writer's position in the following example?**

> Although it is claimed that working from home can encourage time-wasting due to domestic distractions, research indicates that the vast majority of homeworkers are conscientious and productive, completing tasks on time, perhaps due to the absence of office activity.

■ **Study the example below, and write two more similar sentences on the topic of homeworking.**

Counterargument	Your position
Some people believe that homeworkers become isolated,	but this can be avoided by holding weekly departmental meetings for all staff.

11 Progress check

■ **Write two paragraphs on the topic: 'Is the exploration of space worthwhile?' Use the ideas below and make your position clear.**

Pros

- Scientists need to collect information to understand universe
- Space engineering has produced many useful discoveries (e.g. satellite communication)

- Exploration promotes cooperation between nations (e.g. space station)

(source: Donnet-Kammel, 2005)

Cons

- Huge amounts of money are spent with little result
- Resources should be spent on urgent needs on earth (e.g. disease control)
- National space programmes are testing potential weapons (e.g. missiles)

(Source: Soroka, 2000)

Avoiding Plagiarism/ Giving Examples

In the English-speaking academic world, it is essential to use a wide range of sources for your writing, and to acknowledge these sources clearly. This unit introduces the techniques students need to do this, in order to avoid the risk of plagiarism.

Effective writers give examples for support and illustration. Suitable examples can strengthen the argument, and they can also help the reader to understand a point. This unit demonstrates the different ways in which examples can be introduced, and practises their use.

PROCESS: AVOIDING PLAGIARISM

1 What is plagiarism?

In academic work, ideas and words are seen as private property belonging to the person who first thought or wrote them. Plagiarism means taking ideas or words from a source, such as a book or journal, without giving credit (acknowledgement) to the author. It is seen as a kind of theft, and is considered to be an academic crime. Therefore, it is important for all students, including international ones, to understand the meaning of plagiarism and learn how to prevent it in their work.

Why students must avoid plagiarism:

* To show that they understand the rules of the academic community
* Copying the work of others will not help them develop their own understanding

- Plagiarism is easily detected by teachers and computer software
- Plagiarism may lead to failing a course or even having to leave college

2 Acknowledging sources

If you borrow from or refer to the work of another person, you must show that you have done this by providing the correct acknowledgement. There are two ways to do this:

Summary and citation

> *Smith (2009) claims that the modern state exercises power in new ways.*

Quotation and citation

> *According to Smith: 'The point is not that the state is in retreat but that it is developing new forms of power . . .' (Smith, 2009:103).*

These in-text **citations** are linked to a list of **references** at the end of the main text, which includes the following details:

Author	Date	Title	Place of publication	Publisher
Smith, M.	(2009)	*Power and the State*	Basingstoke:	Palgrave Macmillan

The citation makes it clear to the reader that you have read Smith and borrowed this idea from him. The reference gives the reader the necessary information to find the source if the reader needs more detail.

3 Degrees of plagiarism

Although plagiarism essentially means copying somebody else's work, it is not always easy to define.

■ **Working with a partner, consider the following academic situations and decide if they are plagiarism.**

	Situation	Plagiarism? Yes/No
1	Copying a paragraph from a book, but changing a few words and giving a citation.	
2	Cutting and pasting a short article from a website, with no citation.	
3	Taking a graph from a textbook, giving the source.	
4	Taking a quotation from a source, giving a citation but not using quotation marks.	
5	Using something that you think of as general knowledge (e.g. the level of carbon dioxide – CO_2 – in the atmosphere is increasing).	
6	Using the results of your own research (e.g. from a survey you did), without citation.	
7	Discussing an essay topic with a group of classmates and using some of their ideas in your own work.	

This exercise shows that plagiarism can be accidental. For example, situation 4 above, where there are no quotation marks, is technically plagiarism but really carelessness. In situation 7, your teacher may have told you to discuss the topic in groups, and then write an essay on your own, in which case it would not be plagiarism. It can be difficult to decide what is general or common knowledge (situation 5), but you can always try asking colleagues.

However, it is not a good excuse to say that you didn't know the rules of plagiarism, or that you didn't have time to write in your own words. Nor is it adequate to say that the rules are different in your own country. In general, anything that is not common knowledge or your own ideas and research (published or not) must be cited and referenced.

4 Avoiding plagiarism by summarising and paraphrasing

Quotations should not be overused, so you must learn to paraphrase and summarise in order to include other writers' ideas in your work. This will demonstrate your understanding of a text.

- **Paraphrasing** involves rewriting a text so that the language is significantly different while the content stays the same.
- **Summarising** means reducing the length of a text but retaining the main points.

Normally, both skills are used at the same time, as can be seen in the examples below.

■ Read the following text and then compare the paragraphs below, which use ideas and information from it. Decide which are plagiarised and which are acceptable, giving your reasons.

RAILWAY MANIAS

In 1830 there were a few dozen miles of railways in all the world – chiefly consisting of the line from Liverpool to Manchester. By 1840 there were over 4,500 miles, by 1850 over 23,500. Most of them were projected in a few bursts of speculative frenzy known as the 'railway manias' of 1835–7 and especially in 1844–7; most of them were built in large part with British capital, British iron, machines and know-how. These investment booms appear irrational, because in fact few railways were much more profitable to the investor than other forms of enterprise, most yielded quite modest profits and many none at all: in 1855 the average interest on capital sunk in the British railways was a mere 3.7 per cent.

(*The Age of Revolution* by Eric Hobsbawm, 1995, p.45)

---

a)   Between 1830 and 1850 there was very rapid development in railway construction world-wide. Two periods of especially feverish growth, mainly with British involvement, were 1835–7 and 1844–7. It is hard to understand the reason for this intense activity, since railways were not particularly profitable investments and some produced no return at all. (Hobsbawm, 1995:45)

b)   There were only a few dozen miles of railways in 1830, including the Liverpool to Manchester line. But by 1840 there were over 4,500 miles and over 23,500 by 1850. Most of them were built in large part with

British capital, British iron, machines and know-how, and most of them were projected in a few bursts of speculative frenzy known as the 'railway manias' of 1835–7 and especially in 1844–7. Because most yielded quite modest profits, and many none at all, these investment booms appear irrational. In fact few railways were much more profitable to the investor than other forms of enterprise. (Hobsbawm, 1995:45)

c)   As Hobsbawm (1995) argues, nineteenth century railway mania was partly irrational: 'because in fact few railways were much more profitable to the investor than other forms of enterprise, most yielded quite modest profits and many none at all: in 1855 the average interest on capital sunk in the British railways was a mere 3.7 per cent.' (Hobsbawm, 1995:45)

d)   Globally, railway networks increased dramatically from 1830 to 1850; the majority in short periods of 'mania' (1835–7 and 1844–7). British technology and capital were responsible for much of this growth, yet the returns on the investment were hardly any better than for comparable business opportunities. (Hobsbawm, 1895:45)

	Plagiarised or acceptable?	**Reason**
a)		
b)		
c)		
d)		

5 Avoiding plagiarism by developing good study habits

Few students deliberately try to cheat by plagiarising, but some develop poor study habits that result in the risk of plagiarism.

■ **Working with a partner, add to the list of positive habits.**

• Plan your work carefully so you don't have to write the essay at the last minute.

• Take care to make notes in your own words, not copying from the source.

• _____

SKILLS: GIVING EXAMPLES

6 Introducing examples

Examples are an important element in effective writing. Without examples, writing can seem too theoretical:

> *The overuse of antibiotics has had serious negative consequences.*

An example makes the idea easier to understand:

> *The overuse of antibiotics has had serious negative consequences.* **Hospital-acquired infections such as MRSA have become more difficult to treat and this has resulted in many deaths.**

Generalisations are commonly used to introduce a topic:

> *Many plants and animals are threatened by global warming.*

But if the reader is given an example for illustration, the idea becomes more concrete:

> *Many plants and animals are threatened by global warming.* **Polar bears, for example, are suffering from the lack of Arctic ice.**

7 Phrases to introduce examples

a) **for instance, for example** (with commas)

> *Some car manufacturers, for instance Kia, now offer seven-year guarantees.*

b) **such as, e.g.**

Many successful businessmen such as Bill Gates have no formal qualifications.

c) **particularly, especially** (to give a focus)

Certain Master's courses, especially American ones, take two years.

d) **a case in point** (for single examples)

A few diseases have been successfully eradicated. A case in point is smallpox.

■ **Add a suitable example to each sentence and introduce it with one of the phrases above.**

Example:

A number of sports have become very profitable due to the sale of television rights.

A number of sports, **for instance motor racing**, have become very profitable due to the sale of television rights.

a) Some twentieth-century inventions affected the lives of most people.

b) Lately, many countries have introduced fees for university courses.

c) Various companies have built their reputation on the strength of one product.

d) In recent years, more women have become political leaders.

e) Certain countries are frequently affected by earthquakes.

f) Many musical instruments use strings to make music.

8 Practice

■ **Study the following text and add examples from the box where suitable, using an introductory phrase from section 7 above.**

---

free delivery or discounted prices

bookshops

clothing and footwear

books and music

many supermarkets offer delivery services for online customers

---

THE CHANGING FACE OF SHOPPING

Widespread use of the internet has led to a major change in shopping habits. It is no longer necessary to visit shops to make routine purchases. With more specialised items internet retailers can offer a wider range of products than bricks-and-mortar shops. They can also provide extra incentives to customers, in addition to the convenience of not having to visit a real shop. As a result certain types of store are disappearing from the high street. Other products, however, appear to require personal inspection and approval, and in addition many people enjoy the activity of shopping, so it seems unlikely that the internet will completely replace the shopping centre.

---

9 Restatement

Another small group of phrases is used when there is only one 'example' (brackets may also be used for this purpose). This is a kind of restatement to clarify meaning:

---

in other words   namely   that is (to say)   i.e.   viz. (very formal)

---

*The world's leading gold producer, **namely** South Africa, has been faced with a number of technical difficulties.*

■ Add a suitable phrase from the box opposite to the following sentences, to make them clearer.

a)   The company's overheads doubled last year.

b)   The Roman Empire was a period of autocratic rule.

c)   The Indian capital has a thriving commercial centre.

d)   Survival rates for the most common type of cancer are improving.

e)   Participation rates in most democracies are in decline.

> that is to say fewer people are voting   (27 BC–AD 476)
>
> in other words the fixed costs   namely New Delhi
>
> i.e. breast cancer

10 Progress check

■ Read the text below and then insert suitable examples where needed to illustrate the points.

A NEW PERSPECTIVE?

Students who go to study abroad often experience a type of culture shock when they arrive in the new country. Customs which they took for granted in their own society may not be followed in the host country. Even everyday patterns of life may be different. When these are added to the inevitable differences which occur in every country students may at first feel confused. They may experience rapid changes of mood, or even want to return home. However, most soon make new friends and, in a relatively short period, are able to adjust to their new environment. They may even find that they prefer some aspects of their new surroundings, and forget that they are not at home for a while!

Understanding Titles and Essay Planning/Showing Cause and Effect

It is essential for students to understand what an essay title is asking them to do. A plan can then be prepared to ensure the question is answered fully. This unit looks at:

- key words in titles
- essay length and organisation
- alternative methods of essay planning
- two methods of showing the link between a cause (e.g. a cold winter) and an effect (e.g. an increase in illness)

PROCESS: UNDERSTANDING TITLES AND ESSAY PLANNING

1 The planning process

Teachers frequently complain that students do not answer the question set, but this can be avoided by more care at the start of the process: the planning stage. Planning is necessary with all academic writing, but clearly there are important differences between planning in exams, when time is short, and for coursework, when preparatory reading is required. However, in both cases, the process of planning should include these three steps:

a) Analyse the title wording.

b) Decide how long each section should be.

c) Prepare an outline using your favourite method.

2 Analysing essay titles

Titles contain key words that tell students what to do:

'**What** is meant by a demand curve and **why** would we expect it to slope downwards?'

Note that titles often have two (or more) parts. In this case, 'what' is asking for a description and 'why' for a reason or explanation.

■ **Match the key words on the left to the definitions on the right.**

Analyse	Give examples
Assess/Evaluate	Deal with a complex subject by reducing it to the main elements
Describe	Divide into sections and discuss each critically
Discuss	Break down into the various parts and their relationships
Examine/Explore	Make a proposal and support it
Illustrate	Look at various aspects of a topic, compare benefits and drawbacks
Outline/Trace	Give a detailed account of something
Suggest	**Explain a topic briefly and clearly**
Summarise	Decide the value or worth of a subject

3 Practice A

■ **Underline the key words in the following titles and consider what they are asking for.**

a) Summarise the main reasons for the growth of e-commerce, and discuss the likely results of this.

b) Describe some of the reasons why patients do not always take their medication as directed.

c) What are the benefits of learning a second language at primary school (age 6–10)? Are there any drawbacks to early language learning?

d) What are the most significant sources of renewable energy? Evaluate their contribution to the reduction of carbon emissions.

4 Brainstorming

It is often helpful to start thinking about a topic by writing down the ideas you have, in any order. Taking the example from 3a above, you might collect the following points:

Growth of e-commerce – likely results

Main reasons

- Businesses can offer a wider range of products via internet
- More convenient for customers than travelling to shops
- Businesses can reduce overheads by centralising distribution centres
- Prices can often be lower

Likely results

- Growth in delivery businesses
- Decline in conventional shops
- Shopping centres become entertainment areas

■ **Working with a partner, brainstorm ideas for the title from 3c above.**

5 Essay length

Coursework essays usually have a required length, normally between 1,000 and 5,000 words. You must keep to this limit, although 5 per cent more or less is generally acceptable. However, at the planning stage, you need to consider what proportion of the essay to give to each part of the question.

As a basic guide, 20 per cent is usually sufficient for the introduction and conclusion together (references are not included in the word count). Therefore, in a 2,000-word essay, the introduction and conclusion would have 400 words and the main body 1,600 words.

If title 3a above was 2,000 words in total, you might decide on the following allocation:

Main reasons – benefits for buyers	500 words
benefits for sellers	300 words
Likely results – for businesses	400 words
for urban development	400 words
Total	1,600 words

This calculation is useful since it can guide the amount of reading you need to do, as well as providing the basis for an outline. Moreover, it prevents you from writing an unbalanced answer, in which part of the question is not fully dealt with.

Essays in exams do not have a word limit, but it is equally important to plan them in similar terms (e.g. part 1: 40 per cent, part 2: 60 per cent).

■ **Study the following titles and decide what percentage of the main body to give to each part.**

Title	Part 1 (%)	Part 2 (%)
a) How can schools make better use of IT (information technology)? Illustrate your answer with examples.		
b) What are the benefits of learning a second language at primary school (age 6–10)? Are there any drawbacks to early language learning?		
c) What are the most significant sources of renewable energy? Evaluate their contribution to the reduction of carbon emissions.		

6 Outlines/plans

An outline should help the writer to answer the question as effectively as possible. Care at this stage will save wasted effort later. The more detail you include in your outline, the easier the writing process will be. Note that for coursework, it is usually better to write the main body first, then the introduction and finally the conclusion. Therefore, you may prefer to outline just the main body at this stage.

There is no fixed pattern for an outline; different methods appeal to different students. For example, with the first part of title 3a:

'Summarise the main reasons for the growth of e-commerce'

a)   The outline might be a list:

<u>1. Benefits for buyers</u>
- greater convenience in shopping by computer at any time
- lower prices
- better choice

<u>2. Benefits for sellers</u>
- cost saving by centralising distribution
- global customer base
- 24/7 trading

b)   An alternative is a mind map:

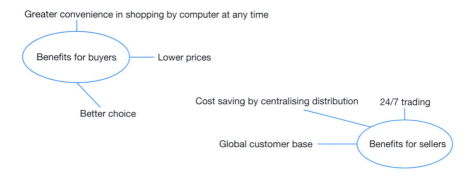

■   **Discuss the advantages and drawbacks of each method with a partner.**

SKILLS: SHOWING CAUSE AND EFFECT

7 The language of cause and effect

Many essay topics require a writer to show the link between a cause, such as the growth of e-commerce, and an effect, such as fewer shops on the high street. Writers may choose to emphasise the cause or the effect. In either case, verbs or conjunctions can be used to show the link.

a) **Focus on causes**

With verbs

The heavy rain	*caused*	*the flood*
	led to	
	resulted in	

With conjunctions

Because of	**the heavy rain**	*there was a flood*
Due to		
As a result of		

b) **Focus on effects**

With verbs (note use of passives)

The flood	*was caused by*	*the heavy rain*
	was produced by	
	resulted from	

With conjunctions

*There was **a flood***	*due to*	*the heavy rain*
	because of	
	as a result of	

Compare the following:

***Because** children **were vaccinated** diseases declined.* (because + verb)

***Because** of the **vaccination** diseases declined.*   (because of + noun)

***As/since** children **were vaccinated** diseases declined.* (conjunction + verb)

***Owing to/due to** the **vaccination** diseases declined.* (conjunction + noun)

8 Practice B

■ Match the causes with their likely effects and then write sentences linking them together, focusing either on the cause or the effect.

Causes	Effects
a) Cold winter of 2012	stores closing on high street
b) Higher rates of literacy	a new government formed
c) Last year's national election	greater demand for secondary education
d) Installing speed camera on main roads	increased demand for electricity
e) Opening a new hospital	a fall in the number of fatal accidents
f) More people shopping on internet	reduced infant mortality

Example: a) Owing to the cold winter of 2012, there was increased demand for electricity.

9 Practice C

■ Use conjunctions to complete the following paragraph.

Why women live longer

Some British scientists now believe that women live longer than men

a) _____ T cells, a vital part of the immune system that protects the body from diseases. Previously, various theories have attempted to explain longer female life expectancy. Biologists claimed that women lived longer b) _____ they need to bring up children. Others argued that men take more risks,

c) _____ they die earlier. But a team from Imperial College think that the difference may be d) _____ women having better immune systems. Having studied a group of men and women they found that the body produces fewer T cells as it gets older,

e) _____ the ageing process. However, they admit that

this may not be the only factor, and f) _____ another

research project may be conducted.

10 Progress check

■ Study the flow chart below, which shows some of the possible effects of a
higher oil price. Complete the paragraph describing this situation, including
examples where suitable.

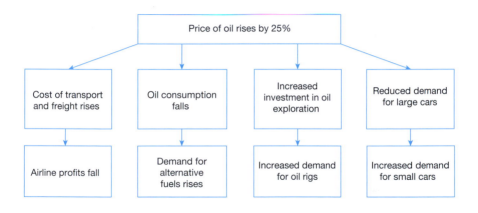

An increase of 25% in the price of oil would have various likely results. First, it might lead to . . .

■ Choose a similar situation in your own subject area. Draw a flow chart
showing some probable effects, and write a paragraph to describe them.

UNIT 1.6 Finding Key Points and Note-Making/Using Abbreviations

After finding suitable sources and preparing an outline, the next step is to select the key points in the sources that relate to your topic, and make notes on them. This unit explains and practises this process, and also demonstrates the use of abbreviations in note-making and other types of academic writing.

PROCESS: FINDING KEY POINTS AND NOTE-MAKING

1 Why make notes?

Making notes is a common activity, but in academic work it is a vital stage of the writing process. International students should learn to make notes in English to improve their overall writing efficiency.

■ **What are the main reasons for note-making? Discuss with a partner and add to the list.**

- *To prepare for essay writing* _____
- _____
- _____
- _____
- _____
- _____

2 Note-making methods

■ **You are looking for information on the current media revolution. Study the text (key points underlined) and the notes in the box on p. 50. What do you notice about the language of the notes?**

THE DEATH OF THE PRESS?

A hundred years ago news was exclusively provided by newspapers. There was no other way of supplying the latest information on politics, crime, finance or sport to the millions of people who bought and read newspapers, sometimes twice a day. Today the situation is very different. The same news is also available on television, radio and the internet, and because of the nature of these media, can be more up-to-date than in print. For young people especially, the internet has become the natural source of news and comment.

This development means that in many countries newspaper circulation is falling, and a loss of readers also means a fall in advertising, which is the main income for most papers. Consequently, in both Britain and the USA newspapers are closing every week. But when a local newspaper goes out of business an important part of the community is lost. It allows debate on local issues, as well as providing a noticeboard for events such as weddings and society meetings.

All newspapers are concerned by these developments, and many have tried to find methods of increasing their sales. One approach is to focus on magazine-type articles rather than news, another is to give free gifts such as DVDs, while others have developed their own websites to provide continuous news coverage. However, as so much is now freely available online to anyone with a web browser, none of these have had a significant impact on the steady decline of paid-for newspapers.

(Source: *New Business Monthly*, May 2013, p. 37)

Decline of newspapers   (*New Business Monthly*, May 2013, p. 37)

a)   Newspapers only source of news 100 yrs ago – now also TV, radio + www

b)   Newspaper   decline in   UK and US
     sales   >   advertising   >   newspapers closing

c)   Attempts to attract readers: •   more magazine content

                                         •   free gifts

                                         •   websites

d)   but none very effective

---

3 Effective note-making

Notes are for your personal use so you should create your own style. Your teachers will not read or mark them, but you need to make sure you can still understand your notes months after reading the original book or article.

a)   To avoid the risk of plagiarism, you must use your own words and not copy phrases from the original. The quantity of notes you make depends on your task: you may only need a few points, or a lot of detail.

b)   Always record the source of your notes. This will save time when you have to write the list of references.

c)   Notes are often written quickly, so keep them simple. Do not write sentences. Leave out articles (a/the) and prepositions (of/to).

d)   If you write lists, it is important to have clear headings (underlined) and numbering systems (a, b, c, or 1, 2, 3) to organise the information. Do not crowd your notes.

e)   Use symbols (+, >, =) to save time.

f)   Use abbreviations (see section 6 below). You need to make up your own abbreviations for your subject area. But do not abbreviate too much, or you may find your notes hard to understand in the future!

4 Finding relevant points

When preparing to write an essay, you have to search for information and ideas linked to your subject. Therefore, the points that you select to note must relate directly to that topic.

■ You are given an essay title: 'Does the state have a role in promoting public health?' Read the following article and underline the key points that relate to your essay subject (the first one has been done for you).

A SLIMMER AMERICA?

In the USA there has recently been more pressure for informative food labelling, and government campaigns to encourage school children to eat more fruit and vegetables. Although Americans often dislike being told what to do by their government, these campaigns may finally be having an effect. Certainly about a third of the population attempt a slimming programme every year, and although many give up, it appears that the number of people who succeed may be rising.

Currently over two-thirds of Americans are believed to be either overweight or obese, but recently it has been discovered that the situation may have stabilised. The rate of increase appears to have virtually stopped, so that on average women and children weigh no more now than they did ten years ago. This trend may have important consequences for the health care system: according to a recent study (Finkelstein *et al.*, 2009) an obese American is likely to cost the system over 40% more than someone with normal weight. This is due to the increased risks of medical conditions such as diabetes, to which should be added extra costs connected with illness and resulting absence from work.

Until recently it was assumed that the long-term trend would continue, so that ultimately all Americans would become overweight; Wang (2008) had estimated that this would happen by 2048. Obviously, such an assumption implies steadily rising medical insurance costs. If the new trend continues there are clear benefits for public health and the associated finances, but medical researchers still struggle to understand the basic causes of the problem, which is that obesity in America is now three times greater than fifty years ago.

There is substantial evidence that obesity is linked to social class: those with irregular and badly paid employment are more likely to eat what is convenient and tasty rather than have the time or energy to organise a healthy diet. The number of people in this category may have risen in recent years. Another possibility is that food now is cheaper relative to income, while free time is more valuable, so people are attracted to consuming convenient but often unhealthy fast food. In addition, washing machines and other devices mean that people use fewer calories doing domestic chores around the house.

(Herapath, T. (2012) *Journal of Transatlantic Contexts* 14, p. 319)

5 Practice A

■ Complete the notes for 'Does the state have a role in promoting public health?' using the key points underlined above.

Source: (Herapath, T. (2012) *Journal of Transatlantic Contexts* 14, p. 319)

<u>Have Americans stopped getting fatter?</u>

1)   US govt. efforts to encourage healthy eating may be succeeding

2)   _____

3)   _____

4)   _____

SKILLS: USING ABBREVIATIONS

6 Types of abbreviations

Abbreviations are an important and expanding feature of contemporary English, widely used for convenience and space saving. Students need to be familiar with general and academic abbreviations. Abbreviations take the form of shortened words, acronyms and other abbreviations, as shown below.

a)   **Shortened words** are often used without the writer being aware of the original form: 'lab' for 'laboratory' and 'memo' for 'memorandum' are now quite standard.

b)   **Acronyms** are made up of the initial letters of a name or phrase (e.g. AIDS = Acquired Immune Deficiency Syndrome). They are pronounced as words.

c) **Other abbreviations** are read as sets of individual letters. They include names of countries, organisations and companies (USA/BBC), and also abbreviations that are only found in written English (e.g. PTO means 'please turn over'). Note that in many cases, abbreviations are widely used without most users knowing what the individual letters stand for (e.g. DNA, DVD).

7 Common academic abbreviations

BA	Bachelor of Arts
BCE	before common era (in dates)
BSc	Bachelor of Sciences
CV	curriculum vitae
EU	European Union
FE	further education (non-university study after school)
GM	genetically modified
GNP	gross national product
HE	higher education (university study above 18)
HRM	human resource management
ICT	information and communications technology
LLB	Bachelor of Laws
MA	Master of Arts
MSc	Master of Science
PG	Postgraduate
PGCE	Postgraduate Certificate of Education
PhD	Doctor of Philosophy
UCAS	Universities and Colleges Admissions Service
UG	undergraduate
URL	uniform resource locator (website address)
VC	Vice-Chancellor

However, writers also employ more specialised abbreviations in texts, which are explained on first use:

> *The Technology Readiness Index (TRI) was introduced by Parasuraman (2000).*

8 Abbreviations in writing

While many academic subjects have their own abbreviations, there are certain abbreviations common to all types of academic writing. They include:

anon.   anonymous (no author)

asap	as soon as possible
c.	circa (in dates = about)
cf.	compare
ed.	editor/edition
e.g.	for example
et al.	and others (used in citations for multiple authors)
etc.	et cetera (and so on – do not use this in academic work)
Fig.	figure (for labelling charts and graphs)
ibid.	in the same place (to refer to a source mentioned immediately before)
i.e.	that is
K	thousand
NB.	take careful note
nd.	no date (i.e. an undated source)
op. cit.	in the source mentioned previously
p.a.	yearly (per annum)
pp.	pages
PS	postscript
re.	with reference to
sic	used to show that a quoted word appears incorrect to the writer
vs	versus

9 Practice B

■ Explain the abbreviations in the following sentences.

a) The failure rate among ICT projects in HE reaches 40% (Smith *et al.*, 2008).

b) GM technology is leading to advances in many fields e.g. forestry.

c) NB. CVs must be submitted to HRM by June 30th.

d) The city seems to have been destroyed c.2500 BCE.

e) Her PhD examined the spread of malaria in SE Asia.

f) Fig.4. Trade patterns on the www (2008–2014).

g) The VC is meeting the PGCE students.

h) Prof. Wren asked for the report asap.

10 Progress check

■ You have to write an essay titled: 'Improving student performance: an outline of recent research.' Read the following text, underline the relevant key points and make notes on them.

SLEEP AND MEMORY

In many countries, especially in hot climates, it is the custom to take a short sleep in the afternoon, often known as a siesta. Now it appears that this habit helps to improve the ability to remember and therefore to learn. Researchers have known for some time that new memories are stored short-term in an area of the brain called the hippocampus, but are then transferred to the pre-frontal cortex for long-term storage. They now believe that this transfer process occurs during a kind of sleep called stage 2 non-REM sleep. After this has occurred the brain is better able to take in new information, and having a sleep of about 100 minutes after lunch seems to be an effective way to allow this.

Research by a team from the University of California sought to confirm this theory. They wanted to establish that a short sleep would restore the brain's ability to learn. A group of about 40 people were asked to take part in two 'lessons'; at 12 noon and 6 pm. Half the volunteers were put in a group which stayed awake all day, while the others were encouraged to sleep for an hour and a half after the first session. It was found that in the evening lesson the second group were better at remembering what they had learnt, which indicates that the siesta had helped to refresh their short-term memories.

(Kitschelt, P. (2006) *How the Brain Works*. Berlin: Freihaus p.73)

UNIT 1.7 Summarising and Paraphrasing/ Finding Synonyms

Summarising and paraphrasing are normally used together in essay writing. Summarising aims to condense information to a suitable length, while paraphrasing means changing the wording of a text so that it is significantly different from the original source, without changing the meaning. These skills are needed to avoid the risk of plagiarism, and this unit practises them separately and together.

This stage of the writing process requires the use of synonyms, which are different words with a similar meaning. A good writer also uses them to avoid repetition and thus provide more interest for the reader. This unit provides examples of common synonyms in academic writing.

PROCESS: SUMMARISING AND PARAPHRASING

1 Successful summarising

Summarising is a common activity in everyday life, used to describe the main features of the subject.

■ Write a short description of a film you have recently watched, in about 20 words.

_____

_____

_____

_____

■ **Compare your summary with others in your class. Discuss what is needed for a good summary.**

- _____
- _____
- _____

Summarising is a flexible tool, allowing the writer to condense lengthy sources into a concise form. You can use it to give a one-sentence outline of an article, or to provide much more detail, depending on your needs. But generally, a summary focuses on the main ideas and excludes examples or supporting information. In every case, the same basic steps need to be followed in order to meet the criteria discussed above.

■ **Study the stages of summary writing below, which have been mixed up. Put them in the correct order (1–5).**

a)   Write the summary from your notes, reorganising the structure if needed.

b)   Make notes of the key points, paraphrasing where possible.

c)   Read the original text carefully and check any new or difficult vocabulary.

d)   Mark the key points by underlining or highlighting.

e)   Check the summary to ensure it is accurate and nothing important has been changed or lost.

2 Practice A

■ **Read the following text and the summaries that follow. Which is best? Give reasons.**

MECHANICAL PICKERS

Although harvesting cereal crops such as wheat and barley has been done for many years by large machines known as combine harvesters, mechanising the picking of fruit crops such as tomatoes or apples has proved more difficult. Farmers have generally relied on human labour to harvest these, but in wealthy countries it has become increasingly difficult to find people willing to work for the wages farmers are able to pay. This is partly because the demand for labour is seasonal, usually in the autumn, and also because the work is hard. As a result, in areas such as California part of the fruit harvest is often unpicked and left to rot.

There are several obvious reasons why developing mechanical pickers is challenging. Fruit such as grapes or strawberries comes in a variety of shapes and does not always ripen at the same time. Outdoors, the ground conditions can vary from dry to muddy, and wind may move branches around. Clearly each crop requires its own solution: machines may be pulled through orchards by tractors or move around by themselves, using sensors to detect the ripest fruit.

This new generation of fruit harvesters is possible due to advances in computing power and sensing ability. Such devices will inevitably be expensive, but will save farmers from the difficulty of managing a labour force. In addition, the more intelligent pickers should be able to develop a database of information on the health of each individual plant, enabling the grower to provide it with fertiliser and water to maintain its maximum productivity.

a) Fruit crops have usually been picked by hand, as it is difficult to mechanise the process owing to natural variables. But in rich countries it has become hard to find affordable pickers at the right time, so fruit is often wasted. Therefore intelligent machines have been developed which can overcome the technical problems involved, and also provide farmers with useful data about the plants.

b) Developing machines that can pick fruit such as tomatoes or apples is a challenging task, due to the complexity of locating ripe fruit in an unpredictable outdoor environment, where difficult conditions can be produced by wind, heat or water. But recent developments in computing ability mean that growers can now automate this process, which should save them money and increase their profits.

3 Practice B

■ a) Read the following text and underline the key points.

WEALTH AND FERTILITY

For most of the past century an inverse correlation between human fertility and economic development has been found. This means that as a country got richer, the average number of children born to each woman got smaller. While in the poorest countries women often have eight children, the rate fell as low as 1.3 children per woman in some European countries such as Italy, which is below the replacement rate. Such a low rate has two likely negative consequences: the population will fall in the long-term, and a growing number of old people will have to be supported by a shrinking number of young.

But a recent study by researchers from Pennsylvania University suggests that this pattern may be changing. They related a country's fertility rates to its economic and social development. In the majority of advanced nations the fertility rate has started to increase, and in some is approaching two children per woman. Although there are exceptions such as Japan, it appears that rising levels of wealth and education eventually translate into a desire for more children.

■ b) Complete the notes of the key points below.

i)   Falling levels of fertility have generally been found _____.

ii)   In some, number of children born _____.

iii) Two results: smaller populations and _____.

iv)   Recent research claims that _____.

v)   In most advanced countries _____.

■ c) Join the notes together and expand them to make the final summary.
   Check that the meaning is clear and no important points have been left out.
   Find a suitable title.

■ **d)** This summary is about 35% of the original length, but it could be summarised further. Summarise the summary in no more than 20 words.

4 Practice C

■ Summarise the following text in about 50 words.

THE LAST WORD IN LAVATORIES?

Toto is a leading Japanese manufacturer of bathroom ceramic ware, with annual worldwide sales of around $5 bn. One of its best-selling ranges is the Washlet lavatory, priced at up to $5,000 and used in most Japanese homes. This has features such as a heated seat, and can play a range of sounds. This type of toilet is successful in its home market since many Japanese flats are small and crowded, and bathrooms provide valued privacy. Now Toto hopes to increase its sales in Europe and America, where it faces a variety of difficulties. European countries tend to have their own rules about lavatory design, so that different models have to be made for each market. Although Toto claims that its Washlet toilet uses less water than the average model, one factor which may delay its advance into Europe is its need for an electrical socket for installation, as these are prohibited in bathrooms by most European building regulations.

---

5 Paraphrasing

Paraphrasing and summarising are normally used together in essay writing, but while summarising aims to **reduce** information to a suitable length, paraphrasing attempts to **restate** the relevant information. For example, the following sentence:

> *There has been much debate about the reasons for the industrial revolution happening in eighteenth-century Britain, rather than in France or Germany.*

could be paraphrased:

> *Why the industrial revolution occurred in Britain in the eighteenth century, instead of on the continent, has been the subject of considerable discussion.*

Note that an effective paraphrase usually:

- has a different structure to the original
- has mainly different vocabulary
- retains the same meaning
- keeps some phrases from the original that are in common use (e.g. 'industrial revolution' or 'eighteenth century')

6 Practice D

■ Read the text below and then rank the three paraphrases in order 1 (best) to 3, giving reasons.

THE CAUSES OF THE INDUSTRIAL REVOLUTION

Allen (2009) argues that the best explanation for the British location of the industrial revolution is found by studying demand factors. By the early eighteenth century high wages and cheap energy were both features of the British economy. Consequently, the mechanisation of industry through such inventions as the steam engine and mechanical spinning was profitable because employers were able to economise on labour by spending on coal. At that time, no other country had this particular combination of expensive labour and abundant fuel.

a) A focus on demand may help to explain the UK origin of the industrial revolution. At that time workers' pay was high, but energy from coal was inexpensive. This encouraged the development of mechanical inventions based on steam power, which enabled bosses to save money by mechanising production (Allen, 2009).

b) The reason why Britain was the birthplace of the industrial revolution can be understood by analysing demand in the early 1700s, according to Allen (2009). He maintains that, uniquely, Britain had the critical combination of cheap energy from coal and high labour costs. This encouraged the adoption of steam power to mechanise production, thus saving on wages and increasing profitability.

c) Allen (2009) claims that the clearest explanation for the UK location of the industrial revolution is seen by examining demand factors. By the eighteenth century cheap energy and high wages were both aspects of the British economy. As a result, the mechanisation of industry through inventions such as the steam engine and mechanical spinning was profitable because employers were able to save money on employees by spending on coal. At that time, Britain was the only country with significant deposits of coal.

	Reasons
1	
2	
3	

7 Techniques for paraphrasing

a) Changing vocabulary by using synonyms:

argues > claims/eighteenth century > 1700s/wages > labour costs/economise > saving

b) Changing word class:

explanation (n.) > explain (v.)/ mechanical (adj.) > mechanise (v.)/ profitable (adj.) > profitability (n.)

c) Changing word order:

. . . the best explanation for the British location of the industrial revolution is found by studying demand factors > A focus on demand may help explain the UK origin of the industrial revolution.

Note that in practice, all these three techniques are used at the same time.

8 Practice E

■ Read the following text.

BRAINS AND GENDER

It is widely agreed that men and women think and act in different ways. Women appear to have better memories, better social skills and are more competent at multi-tasking. Men, in contrast, seem to focus better on single issues and have superior motor and spatial skills, although clearly many people are exceptions to these patterns.

The differences have been explained as behaviour adopted thousands of years ago, when the men went hunting while the women stayed at home and cared for their children. But another approach is to see the behaviour as a result of the way our brains function. Recent research by Ragini Verma's team at the University of Pennsylvania has used brain scans to compare 428 men and 521 women. They tracked the pathways of water molecules around the brain area, and found fascinating differences.

The top half of the brain is called the cerebrum, and it is divided into a left and a right half. The left hemisphere is thought to be the home of logic and the right is the centre of intuition. Dr Verma found that with women most of the pathways went between the two halves, while with men they stayed inside the hemispheres. She believes that these results explain the gender differences in ability, such as women's social competence compared to men's more intense focus on a limited area.

■ a) Find synonyms for the words underlined. Rewrite the paragraph using these.

It is <u>widely agreed</u> that <u>men and women</u> think and <u>act</u> in different ways. Women <u>appear</u> to have <u>better</u> memories, better social <u>skills</u> and are more <u>competent</u> at multi-tasking. Men, <u>in contrast</u>, seem to focus better on <u>issues</u> and have superior motor and spatial <u>skills</u>, although <u>clearly</u> many people <u>are exceptions to</u> these patterns.

■ **b) Change the word class of the underlined words. Rewrite the paragraph using the changes.**

These differences <u>have been explained</u> as <u>behaviour</u> adopted thousands of years ago, when the men <u>went hunting</u> while the women stayed at home and <u>cared</u> for their children. But another approach is to see the behaviour as <u>a result of</u> the way our brains function.

■ **c) Change the word order of these sentences, rewriting the paragraph so that the meaning stays the same.**

Recent research into brain functioning by Ragini Verma's team at the University of Pennsylvania has used brain scans to compare 428 men and 521 women. They tracked the pathways of water molecules around the brain area, and found fascinating differences.

■ **d) Combine all three techniques to paraphrase the final paragraph of the text.**

SKILLS: FINDING SYNONYMS

9 How synonyms work

The exercises above have demonstrated the importance of synonyms. This section provides further examples and practises their use.

■ **Underline the synonyms in the following text and complete the table.**

Royal Dutch Shell is the **largest** oil company in the world by revenue, with a significant share of the global hydrocarbon market. The **giant** firm employs over 100,000 people internationally, including over 8,000 employees in Britain.

Word/phrase	Synonym
largest	*giant*
oil	
company	
in the world	
people	

a) Synonyms are not always exactly the same in meaning, and it is important not to change the register. 'Firm' is a good synonym for 'company', but 'boss' is too informal to use for 'manager'.

b) Many common words (e.g. culture, economy or industry) have no effective synonyms.

10 Common synonyms in academic writing

■ Match the synonyms in each list.

Nouns		Verbs	
area	advantage	accelerate	**change**
authority	part	**alter**	help
behaviour	argument	analyse	question
benefit	disadvantage	assist	explain
category	tendency	attach	evolve
component	**field**	challenge	examine
controversy	source	clarify	establish
drawback	emotion	concentrate on	insist
expansion	target	confine	speed up
feeling	explanation	develop	take apart
framework	conduct	evaluate	join
goal	topic	found	decrease
interpretation	possibility	maintain	demonstrate
issue	production	predict	increase
method	research	prohibit	cite
option	increase	quote	reinforce
quotation	citation	raise	focus on
results	figures	reduce	forecast
statistics	type	respond	ban
study	structure	retain	limit
trend	system	show	keep
output	findings	strengthen	reply

NB: These pairs are commonly synonymous, but not in every situation.

11 Practice F

■ Find synonyms for the words and phrases underlined, rewriting the sentences where necessary.

a) Professor Hicks <u>questioned</u> the <u>findings</u> of the <u>research</u>.

b) The <u>statistics show</u> a steady <u>increase</u> in applications.

c) The institute's <u>prediction</u> has caused a major <u>controversy</u>.

d) Cost seems to be the <u>leading drawback</u> to that <u>system</u>.

e) They will <u>concentrate on</u> the first <u>option</u>.

f) The <u>framework</u> can be <u>retained</u> but the <u>goal</u> needs to be <u>altered</u>.

g) OPEC, the oil producers' cartel, is to <u>cut production</u> to <u>raise</u> global prices.

h) The <u>trend</u> to smaller families has <u>speeded up</u> in the last decade.

12 Progress check

■ Paraphrase the following text, using synonyms where suitable.

THE PAST BELOW THE WAVES

More than three million shipwrecks are believed to lie on the sea bed, the result of storms and accidents during thousands of years of sea-borne trading. These wrecks offer marine archaeologists valuable information about the culture, technology and trade patterns of ancient civilizations, but the vast majority have been too deep to research. Scuba divers can only operate down to 50 metres, which limits operations to wrecks near the coast, which have often been damaged by storms or plant growth. A few deep sea sites (such as the *Titanic*) have been explored by manned submarines, but this kind of equipment has been too expensive for less famous subjects. However, this situation has been changed by the introduction of a new kind of mini submarine: the automatic underwater vehicle (AUV). This cheap, small craft is free moving and does not need an expensive mother-ship to control it. Now a team of American archaeologists are planning to use an AUV to explore an area of sea north of Egypt, which was the approach to a major trading port 4,000 years ago.

References and Quotations/Using Verbs of Reference

Academic work is based on the research and ideas of others, so it is vital to show which sources you have used in your work, in an acceptable manner. This unit explains:

- the format of in-text citation
- the main reference systems
- the use of quotations
- the layout of lists of references
- the use of verbs of reference

PROCESS: REFERENCES AND QUOTATIONS

1 Why give references?

There are three principal reasons for providing references and citations:

a) To show that you have read some of the authorities on the subject, which will give added weight to your argument.

b) To allow readers to locate your sources, if they wish to examine them in detail.

c) To avoid plagiarism.

It is important to refer correctly to the work of other writers that you have used. As shown in Unit 1.4, you may present these sources as a summary/paraphrase, as a quotation, or use both. In each case, a citation is included to provide a link to the list of references at the end of your paper.

■ Underline the citations in the example below. Which is for a summary and which for a quotation? What are the advantages of each?

> Smith (2009) argues that the popularity of the Sports Utility Vehicle (SUV) is irrational, as despite their high cost most are never driven off-road. In his view 'they are bad for road safety, the environment and road congestion' (Smith, 2009:37).

Using citations

A quotation	Author's name, date of publication, page no.	(Smith, 2009:37)
A summary	Author's name, date of publication	Smith (2009)

2 Reference systems

There are several main systems of referencing employed in the academic world, each used by different subjects. Your teachers will normally give you guidelines, or you may find these on the library website. With any system, the most important point is to be consistent (i.e. to use the same font size, punctuation and capitalisation throughout). These are the principal systems:

a) **The Harvard system**, generally used for the Social Sciences and Business, illustrated above.

b) **The Vancouver system**, widely used in Medicine and Science. Numbers in brackets are inserted after the citation and these link to a numbered list of references:

Jasanoff (5) makes the point that the risk of cross-infection is growing.

> (5) Jasanoff, M. *Tuberculosis: A sub-Saharan perspective*. New York: Schaffter (2001)

c) **The footnote/endnote systems**, commonly used in the Humanities, in which sources are listed either at the bottom of the page or at the end of the paper. The numbers in superscript run consecutively throughout the paper:

The effects of the French Revolution were felt throughout Europe.[3]

---

3 Karl Wildavsky, *The End of an Era: Spain 1785 – 1815* (Dublin: University Press, 2006) p. 69

NB: Referencing is a complex subject and students should use an online reference guide for detailed information. Your university library may provide one, or Sussex University provides a convenient guide to the different systems at:

www.sussex.ac.uk/library/infosuss/referencing/index.shtm

3 Using quotations

■ **Discuss with a partner the reasons for using quotations in your written work.**

Using a quotation means bringing the original words of a writer into your work. Quotations are effective in some situations, but must not be overused (e.g. to 'pad out' your work). They can be valuable:

- when the original words express an idea in a distinctive way
- when the original is more concise than your summary could be
- when the original version is well known

All quotations should be introduced by a phrase that shows the source, and also explains how this quotation fits into your argument:

Introductory phrase	Author	Reference verb	Quotation	Citation
This view is widely shared;	as Friedman	stated:	'Inflation is the one form of taxation that can be imposed without legislation'	(1974: 93).

a) Short quotations (two to three lines) as above are shown by single quotation marks. Quotations inside quotations (nested quotations) use double quotation marks:

As James remarked: 'Martin's concept of "internal space" requires close analysis.'

b) Longer quotations are either indented (given a wider margin) and/or are printed in smaller type. In this case, quotation marks are not needed.

c) Page numbers should be given after the date.

d) Care must be taken to ensure that quotations are the exact words of the original. If it is necessary to delete some words that are irrelevant, use points (. . .) to show where the missing section was:

'Few inventions . . . have been as significant as the mobile phone.'

e) It may be necessary to insert a word or phrase into the quotation to clarify a point. This can be done by using square brackets [ ]:

'Modern ideas [of freedom] differ radically from those of the ancient world.'

4 Practice A

■ Study the following paragraph from an article titled 'The mobile revolution' in the journal 'Development Quarterly' (Issue 34 pages 85–97, 2012) by K. Hoffman. Compare the summary and quotation that follow.

According to recent estimates there are at least 4 billion mobile phones in the world, and the majority of these are owned by people in the developing world. Ownership in the developed world reached saturation level by 2007, so countries such as China, India and Brazil now account for most of the growth. In the poorest countries, with weak transport networks and unreliable postal services, access to telecommunications is a vital tool for starting or developing a business, since it provides access to wider markets. Studies have shown that when household incomes rise, more money is spent on mobile phones than any other item.

a) *Summary*

Hoffman (2012) points out that the main market for mobile phones is now the developing world, and stresses the critical importance of mobile phones for the growth of small businesses there.

b) *Quotation*

According to Hoffman, mobile phone ownership compensates for the weaknesses of infrastructure in the developing world: 'In the poorest countries, with weak transport networks and unreliable postal services, access to telecommunications is a vital tool for starting or developing a business, since it provides access to wider markets' (2012:87).

c)   *Summary and quotation*

Hoffman points out that most of the growth in mobile phone ownership now takes place in the developing world, where it has become crucial for establishing a business: '. . . access to telecommunications is a vital tool for starting or developing a business, since it provides access to wider markets' (2012:87).

■ **Read the next paragraph of the same article, also on p.87.**

In such countries the effect of phone ownership on GDP growth is much stronger than in the developed world, because the ability to make calls is being offered for the first time, rather than as an alternative to existing landlines. As a result, mobile phone operators have emerged in Africa, India and other parts of Asia that are larger and more flexible than Western companies, and which have grown by catering for poorer customers, being therefore well-placed to expand downmarket. In addition Chinese phone makers have successfully challenged the established Western companies in terms of quality as well as innovation.

■ **a) Write a summary of the main point, including a citation.**

■ **b) Introduce a quotation to show the key point, referring to the source.**

■ **c) Combine the summary and the quotation, again acknowledging the source.**

5 Secondary references

It is common to find a reference to an original source in the text you are reading.

For instance, if you are reading a text by Graham you may find:

> *In relation to post-natal infections, Poledna (2008) points out that the rate of infection fell when midwives were literate.*

You may wish to use this information from the original (i.e. Poledna) in your writing, even if you have not read the whole work. This is known as a secondary reference. If it is not possible to locate the original, you can refer to it thus:

> *Poledna (2008)* **cited in Graham (2011:241)** *argued that the rate of infection fell . . .*

You must include the work you have read (i.e. Graham) in the list of references.

6 Organising the list of references

At the end of an essay or report, there must be a list of all the sources cited in the writing. In the Harvard system, illustrated here, the list is organised alphabetically by the family name of the author. You should be clear about the difference between first names and family names. On title pages, the normal format of first name, then family name is used:

> *Sheila Burford, Juan Gonzalez*

But in citations only the family name is used:

> *Burford (2001), Gonzalez (1997)*

In reference lists, use the family name and the initial(s):

> *Burford, S., Gonzalez, J.*

■ **Study the reference list below, from an essay on the effects of age on second language learning, and answer the following questions.**

REFERENCES

Bialystock, E. (1997) 'The structure of age: In search of barriers to second language acquisition', *Second Language Research* 13 (2) 116–137.

Dörnyei, Z. (2009) *The Psychology of Second Language Acquisition*. Oxford: Oxford University Press.

Flege, J. (1999) 'Age of learning and second language speech' in Birdsong, D. (ed.) *Second Language Acquisition and the Critical Period Hypothesis*. London: Lawrence Erlbaum Associates 101–132.

Gass, S. and Selinker, L. (2001) *Second Language Acquisition: An Introductory Course*. London: Lawrence Erlbaum Associates.

Larson-Hall, J. (2008) 'Weighing the benefits of studying a foreign language at a younger starting age in a minimal input situation'. *Second Language Research* 24 (1) 35–63.

Myles, F. (nd) 'Second language acquisition (SLA) research: its significance for learning and teaching issues'. Subject Centre for Languages, Linguistics and Area Studies. http://www.llas.ac.uk/resources/gpg/421. Accessed 1 May 2013.

> The International Commission on Second Language Acquisition (nd)
> 'What is SLA?' http://www.hw.ac.uk/langWWW/icsla/
> icsla.htm#SLA. Accessed 6 May 2013.

a)   Find an example of:

   i)   a book by one author

   ii)   a journal article

   iii) a chapter in an edited book

   iv)   an authored undated website article

   v)   an anonymous webpage

   vi)   a book by two authors

b)   When are italics used?

c)   How are capital letters used in titles?

d)   How is a source with no given author listed?

e)   Write citations for summaries from each of the sources.

> There are many software systems available (e.g. RefWorks or Endnote)
> that automate the making of a list of references. Using one of them not
> only saves time, but may also help to produce a more accurate result.
> Some are free and others require payment, but if you search your
> library website you may find one that you can access without charge.

SKILLS: USING VERBS OF REFERENCE

7 Reference verbs

Summaries and quotations are usually introduced by a reference verb:

Smith (2009) **argues** *that . . .*

Janovic (1972) **claimed** *that . . .*

These verbs can either be in the present or the past tense. Normally, the use of the present tense suggests that the source is recent and still valid, while the past indicates that the source is older and may be out of date, but there are no hard-and-fast rules. In some disciplines, an older source may still be useful.

Reference verbs are used to summarise another writer's approach:

*Previn **argued** that global warming was mainly caused by the solar cycle.*

*Bakewell (1992) **found** that most managers tended to use traditional terms.*

They may also be used to introduce a quotation:

*As Scott **observed**: 'Comment is free but facts are sacred'.*

Most of these verbs are followed by a noun clause beginning with 'that'.

a)   The following mean that the writer is presenting a case:

argue   claim   consider   hypothesise   suggest   believe   think   state

*Melville (2007) **suggested** that eating raw eggs could be harmful.*

b)   A second group describe a reaction to a previously stated position:

accept   admit   agree with   deny   doubt

*Handlesmith **doubts** Melville's suggestion that eating raw eggs . . .*

c)   Others include:

assume   conclude   discover   explain   imply

indicate   maintain   presume   reveal   show

*Patel (2003) **assumes** that inflation will remain low.*

■   Write a sentence referring to what the following writers said (more than one verb may be suitable). Use the past tense.

Example: *Z: 'My research shows that biofuels are environmentally neutral'.*
         *Z **claimed/argued** that biofuels were environmentally neutral.*

a)   A: 'I may have made a mistake in my calculations on energy loss'.

b)   B: 'I did not say that women make better doctors than men'.

c)   C: 'Small firms are more dynamic than large ones'.

d)   D: 'I support C's views on small firms'.

e)   E: 'I'm not sure, but most people probably work to earn money'.

f)   F: 'After much research, I've found that allergies are becoming more common'.

g)   G: 'I think it unlikely that electric cars will replace conventional ones'.

h)   H: 'There may be a link between crime and sunspot activity'.

8 Further referring verbs

A small group of verbs is followed by the pattern:

(somebody/thing + for + noun/gerund):

blame   censure   commend   condemn   criticise

Lee (1998) **blamed** *the media for creating uncertainty.*

NB: All except 'commend' have a negative meaning.

Another group is followed by **(somebody/thing + as + noun/gerund)**:

assess   characterise   classify   define   describe

evaluate   identify   interpret   portray   present

Terry **interprets** *rising oil prices as a result of the Asian recovery.*

■   Rewrite the following statements using verbs from the lists above.

Example: *K: 'Guttman's work is responsible for many of the current social problems'.*
K **blamed** *Guttman's work for many of the current social problems.*

a)   L: 'She was very careless about her research methods'.

b)   M: 'There are four main types of children in care'.

c)   N: 'That company has an excellent record for workplace safety'.

d)   O: 'The noises whales make must be expressions of happiness'.

e)   P: 'Wind power and biomass will be the leading green energy sources'.

f)   Q: 'Darwin was the most influential naturalist of the nineteenth century'.

9 Progress check

■ Read the following book extract and write a summary of about 100 words, including a quotation, with citations. Then write a full reference for the text.

A group of scientists working at Oxford University have been researching the behaviour of crows. Their work shows that the birds appear to be able to make simple tools, a skill which was thought to be unique to man and other primates. In an experiment a piece of meat was placed in a glass tube which was too long for the crow to reach with its beak. The bird was given a length of garden wire, nine cms. long and 0.8 mm. thick, to extract the meat, but it soon discovered that this was not possible if the wire was straight. The bird then held one end of the wire with its feet while it used its beak to bend the other end, making a kind of hook. This could then be used for pulling the meat out of the tube, which in most cases was done within two minutes.

It has been known for some time that chimpanzees use simple tools like sticks to reach food, but it was never thought that crows could show similar levels of intelligence. Eight years ago, however, biologists in the forests of New Caledonia watched crows using sticks to reach insects inside trees. The Oxford experiment was designed to see if the same kind of bird could modify this ability to make a tool out of a material not found in their native forests i.e. wire. According to Professor Kacelnik, one of the scientists involved, the research demonstrates that crows have an understanding of the physical properties of materials and the ability to adapt them for their own uses.

Source: Frank Grummitt, *What Makes Us Human?* (2010) Dublin: Roseberry Press, p. 15

UNIT 1.9

Combining Sources/Providing Cohesion

For most assignments, students are expected to read a range of sources, often containing conflicting views on a topic. In some cases, the contrast between the various views may be the focus of the task. This unit explains how writers can present and organise a range of contrasting sources.

Cohesion means joining a text together with reference words (he, she, theirs) and conjunctions (but, then) so that the whole text is clear and readable. This unit deals with reference words and Unit 1.10 practises conjunctions.

PROCESS: COMBINING SOURCES

1 Mentioning sources

In the early stages of an essay, it is common to refer to the views of other writers on the subject, to show that you are familiar with their work, and that your essay will take their research into account.

■ **Read the following example, from a study of 'technology readiness' in consumers, and answer the questions below.**

The extent to which consumers desire to use new technology is commonly influenced by factors such as consumer attitudes toward specific technologies (Bobbit and Dabholkar, 2001; Curran *et al.*, 2003), the level of technology anxiety exhibited by consumers (Meuter *et al.*, 2003), and consumer capacity and willingness (Walker *et al.*, 2002). Mick and Fournier (1998) argue that consumers can simultaneously exhibit positive feelings (such as intelligence and efficacy) and negative feelings (such as ignorance and ineptitude) towards new technology. Venkatesh (2000) found that 'computer playfulness' and 'computer anxiety' serve as anchors that users employ in forming perceptions of ease of use about new technology.

a)   How many sources are mentioned here?

b)   What was the subject of the research by Meuter *et al.*?

c)   Which source contrasted fear of computers with playing with computers?

d)   Which source examined the paradox of positive and negative attitudes to computers?

e)   How many sources are cited that studied attitudes to particular technologies?

2 Taking a critical approach

It is important to compare a range of views to show that you are familiar with different and conflicting views on a topic. This is because most subjects worth studying are the subject of debate.

■   The two texts below provide different views on the topic of climate change. Read them both and then study the extract (2.3) from an essay that contrasts the two sources. Answer the questions that follow.

2.1 WHY THE EARTH IS HEATING UP

Most scientists now agree that global temperatures have risen over the last century, and that this trend is reflected in such phenomena as the melting of sea ice and the retreat of glaciers. There is a near-consensus that over the period the level of carbon dioxide (CO_2) in the earth's atmosphere has also risen, mainly as a result of burning fossil fuels such as coal and oil. The common view is that the first change is the result of the second; in other words a warmer climate has been caused by the CO_2, which has the effect of trapping the heat from the sun's rays inside the atmosphere; the so-called 'greenhouse effect'. If these theories are accepted it can be expected that temperatures will continue to increase in future as carbon dioxide levels rise, and since this will have harmful effects on agriculture and other human activities, efforts should be made to reduce the burning of fossil fuels.

(Lombardo, 2009)

2.2 DOUBTS ABOUT GLOBAL WARMING

The conventional view that global warming is caused by a rise in carbon dioxide levels has been criticised on a number of grounds. Some critics claim that the recent period of warming is part of a natural cycle of temperature fluctuations which have been recorded over the past few thousand years. They point out that Europe experienced a warm period about 800 years ago which was unrelated to CO_2 levels. Other critics question the reliability of the basic temperature data, and maintain that the apparent rise in temperatures is caused by the growth of cities, regarded as 'heat islands'. In addition some claim that the warming is caused by a reduction in cloud cover, allowing more sunlight to reach the earth's surface. This effect, they believe, is the result of solar activity or sunspots, which are known to fluctuate on an 11-year cycle. As a result of these doubts, climate sceptics argue that there is no need to attempt to reduce the industrial activity that causes carbon dioxide to be produced.

(Wong, 2011)

2.3 HOW STRONG IS THE EVIDENCE FOR GLOBAL WARMING?

Lombardo (2009) puts forward the view that the significant rise in the earth's temperature over the past century is the product of increased levels of atmospheric CO_2 caused by greater use of fossil fuels. He maintains that this position is now generally agreed, and that steps should be taken to reduce future warming by restricting the output of greenhouse gases such as carbon dioxide. However Wong (2011) presents a range of counterarguments. She mentions evidence of historical climate change which cannot have been caused by rising levels of CO_2, and also discusses the difficulty of obtaining reliable data on temperature changes, as well as other claims that solar activity may affect the amount of cloud cover and hence temperature levels. Such uncertainty, she considers, raises doubts about the value of trying to cut CO_2 production.

■ a) 2.3 above summarises ideas from both Lombardo and Wong. Match the examples of summaries in the extract with the original text from 2.1 or 2.2.

Summary	Original
. . . the significant rise in the earth's temperature over the past century is the product of the increased levels of atmospheric CO_2 caused by greater use of fossil fuels.	Example: *There is a near-consensus that over the period the level of carbon dioxide (CO_2) in the earth's atmosphere has also risen, mainly as a result of burning fossil fuels.*
. . . steps should be taken to reduce future warming by restricting the output of greenhouse gases such as carbon dioxide.	
She mentions evidence of historical climate change which cannot have been caused by rising levels of CO_2 . . .	

b) Which verbs are used to introduce the summaries?

c) Which word marks the point where the writer switches from summarising Lombardo to Wong?

d) What other words or phrases could be used at this point?

3 Practice A

■ **Study the three texts below, which reflect different approaches to the topic of globalisation.**

3.1 THE BENEFITS OF GLOBALISATION

It has been argued that globalisation is not a new phenomenon, but has its roots in the age of colonial development in the seventeenth and eighteenth centuries. However, its modern use can be dated to 1983, when Levitt's article 'The Globalisation of Markets' was published. Among the many definitions of the process that have been suggested, perhaps the simplest is that globalisation is the relatively free movement of services, goods, people and ideas world-wide. An indication of the positive effect of the process is that cross-border world trade, as a percentage of global GDP, was 15% in 1990 but is expected to reach 30% by 2017. Among the forces driving globalisation in the last two decades have been market liberalisation, cheap communication via the internet and telephony, and the growth of the BRIC (Brazil, Russia, India and China) economies.

(Costa, 2008)

3.2 GLOBALISATION: THE DOWNSIDE

Considerable hostility to the forces of globalisation has been demonstrated in both the developed and developing worlds. In the former, there is anxiety about the outsourcing of manufacturing and service jobs to countries which offer cheaper labour, while developing countries claim that only a minority have benefited from the increase in world trade. They point out that per-capita income in the 20 poorest countries has hardly changed in the past 40 years, while in the richest 20 it has tripled. The markets of Western nations are still closed to agricultural products from developing countries, and while there is free movement of goods and capital, migration from poor countries to rich ones is tightly controlled.

(Lin, 2006)

3.3 MULTI-NATIONALS AND GLOBALISATION

Multi-national companies have undoubtedly benefited from the relaxation of the import tariff regimes which previously protected local firms, allowing them to operate more freely in markets such as India which have recently liberalised. These corporations have evolved two distinct approaches to the challenge of globalisation. Some, e.g. Gillette, have continued to produce their products in a few large plants with strict control to ensure uniform quality worldwide, while others, for instance Coca-Cola, vary the product to suit local tastes and tend to manufacture their goods on the spot. They claim that an understanding of regional differences is essential for competing with national rivals.

(Brokaw, 2012)

■ **Complete the introductory paragraph from the essay below, using all three sources.**

'Globalisation mainly benefits multi-national companies rather than ordinary people – discuss.'

There is good evidence that globalisation has resulted in a considerable increase in world trade over the past 20-30 years ...

SKILLS: PROVIDING COHESION

4 Reference words

These are used to avoid repetition:

Leonardo da Vinci (1452–1519) was a fifteenth-century Italian genius who produced only a handful of **finished artworks**. However **they**

include **Mona Lisa** and The Last Supper, **the former** perhaps the most famous painting in the world. Although **he** is remembered mainly as an artist, **he** was also an innovative engineer, scientist and anatomist. **His designs** include tanks and flying machines, and although few of **these** were built in **his** lifetime **he** is still remembered as the man who saw **their** possibility.

Here, the reference words function as follows:

Leonardo da Vinci	finished artworks	Mona Lisa	designs
He/His	they	the former	these/their

Examples of reference words and phrases:

Pronouns	he/she/it/they
Possessive pronouns	his/her/hers/its/their/theirs
Objective pronouns	her/him/them
Demonstrative pronouns	this/that/these/those
Other phrases	the former/the latter/the first/ the second/the last

5 Practice B

■ Read the following paragraph and complete the table.

BUSINESS SHORT LIFE

La Ferrera (2007) has researched the life cycle of new businesses. She found that they have an average life of only 4.7 years, and considers this is due to two main reasons; one economic and one social. The former appears to be a lack of capital, the latter a failure to carry out sufficient market research. La Ferrera considers that together these account for approximately 70% of business failures.

Reference	Reference word/phrase
La Ferrera	*She*
new businesses	
average life of only 4.7 years	
one economic	
one social	
the former . . ., the latter . . .	

6 Preventing confusion

To avoid confusing the reader, it is important to use reference words only when the reference is clear and unambiguous. For example:

> *Pablo Picasso moved to Paris in 1904 and worked with George Braque from 1908 to 1909.* **He** *became interested in the analysis of form, which led to cubism.*

In this case, it is not clear which person (Picasso or Braque) 'he' refers to. So to avoid this, write:

> *Pablo Picasso moved to Paris in 1904 and worked with George Braque from 1908 to 1909.* **Picasso** *then became interested in the analysis of form, which led to cubism.*

7 Practice C

■ Read the paragraph below and replace the words in bold with reference words.

Velcro

Velcro is a fabric fastener used with clothes and shoes. **Velcro** was invented by a Swiss engineer called George de Mestral. **Mestral's** idea was derived from studying the tiny hooks found on some plant seeds. **The tiny hooks** cling to animals and help disperse the seeds. Velcro has two sides, one of which is covered in small hooks and the other in loops. When **the hooks and loops** are pressed together they form a strong bond.

Mestral spent eight years perfecting **Mestral's** invention, which **Mestral** called 'Velcro' from the French words 'velour' and 'crochet'. **The invention** was patented in 1955 and today over 60 million metres of Velcro are sold annually.

8 Progress check

■ Use the following information to write a paragraph about the invention of nylon, paying careful attention to the use of reference words.

Nylon

Inventor:	Wallace Carothers
Company:	DuPont Corporation (USA)
Carothers' position:	Director of research centre
Carothers' background:	Chemistry student, specialising in polymers (molecules composed of long chains of atoms)
Properties:	Strong but fine synthetic fibre
Patented:	1935
Mass produced:	1939
Applications:	Stockings, toothbrushes, parachutes, fishing lines, surgical thread

Organising Paragraphs/Using Conjunctions

Paragraphs are the building blocks of academic writing. Well-structured paragraphs help the reader understand the topic more easily by dividing up the argument into convenient sections. Conjunctions are words and phrases which join parts of a sentence together, or link a sentence or paragraph to the next one. Effective reading and writing requires clarity about their use and meaning. This unit looks at:

- the components of paragraphs
- the way the components are linked together
- the linkage between paragraphs in the overall text
- the different functions of conjunctions

PROCESS: ORGANISING PARAGRAPHS

1 Paragraph structure

■ Discuss the following questions with a partner.

- What is a paragraph?

- What is the normal length of a paragraph?

- Is there a standard structure for paragraphs?

■ Study the paragraph below. It is from the introduction to an essay titled: 'Should home ownership be encouraged?'

The rate of home ownership varies widely across the developed world. Germany, for instance, has one of the lowest rates, at 42%, while in

Spain it is twice as high, 85%. Both the USA and Britain have similar rates of about 70%. The reasons for this variation appear to be more cultural and historic than economic, since high rates are found in both rich and poorer countries. There seems to be no conclusive link between national prosperity and the number of home owners.

This paragraph can be analysed thus:

Topic   The rate of home ownership varies widely across the developed world.

Example 1   Germany, **for instance**, has one of the lowest rates, at 42%, **while** in Spain it is twice as high, 85%.

Example 2   **Both** the USA and Britain have similar rates of about 70%.

Reason   **The reasons for** this variation appear to be more cultural and historic than economic, **since** high rates are found in both rich and poorer countries.

Conclusion **There seems to be** no conclusive link between national prosperity and the number of home owners.

This example shows that:

a)   A paragraph is a group of sentences that deal with a single topic. Dividing up a text into paragraphs helps both writers to organise their work and readers to follow the argument more clearly.

b)   The length of paragraphs varies significantly according to text type, but should normally be no less than four or five sentences.

c)   Usually (but not always), the first sentence introduces the topic. Other sentences may give definitions, examples, extra information, reasons, restatements and summaries.

d)   The parts of the paragraph are linked together by the phrases and conjunctions shown in bold above. They act as 'signposts' to guide the reader through the arguments.

2 Practice A

■ **a) Read the next paragraph from the same essay and analyse the paragraph by completing the left-hand column in the table on p. 88 with the following types of sentence:**

Supporting point 1, Supporting point 2, Supporting point 3, Example, Main reason, Topic.

Despite this, many countries encourage the growth of home ownership. Ireland and Spain, for instance, allow mortgage payers to offset payments against income tax. It is widely believed that owning your own home has social as well as economic benefits. Compared to renters, home owners are thought to be more stable members of the community who contribute more to local affairs. In addition, neighbourhoods of owner occupiers are considered to have less crime and better schools. But above all, home ownership encourages saving and allows families to build wealth.

	Despite this, many countries encourage the growth of home ownership.
	Ireland and Spain, for instance, allow mortgage payers to offset payments against income tax.
	It is widely believed that owning your own home has social as well as economic benefits.
Supporting point 1	Compared to renters, home owners are thought to be more stable members of the community who contribute more to local affairs.
	In addition, neighbourhoods of owner occupiers are considered to have less crime and better schools.
	But above all, home ownership encourages saving and allows families to build wealth.

■ b) Underline the words and phrases used to link the sentences together.

■ c) Which phrase is used to link this paragraph to the one before?

3 Development of ideas

■ a) The sentences below form the third paragraph of the same essay, but they have been mixed up. Use the table opposite to put them in the correct order.

i)　When this burst, millions of people lost their homes, which for many had contained their savings.

ii)   These mortgages had been developed to allow higher-risk poorer families to buy their own homes, but this contributed to a property price bubble.

iii) Many economists now argue that there is a maximum level of home ownership which should not be exceeded.

iv)   All these claims were challenged by the economic crash of 2008, which was largely caused by defaults on American sub-prime mortgages.

v)   Even households which had positive equity still felt poorer and reduced their spending.

vi)   Others were trapped in their houses by negative equity, in other words their houses were worth less than they had paid for them.

Topic sentence	*All these claims where challenged by the economic crash of 2008, which was largely caused by defaults on American sub-prime mortgages.*
Definition	
Result 1	
Result 2	
Result 3	
Conclusion	

■ b) Underline the phrase used to link the paragraph to the previous one.

■ c) Underline the words and phrases used to link the sentences together.

4 Introducing paragraphs and linking them together

In order to begin a new topic you may use phrases such as:

> *Turning to the issue of infection rates . . .*

> *Rates of infection must also be examined . . .*

> *Rates of infection is another area for consideration . . .*

Paragraphs can also be introduced with adverbs:

> *Traditionally, few examples were . . .*

> *Finally, the performance of . . .*

> *Currently, there is little evidence of . . .*

In the essay on 'home ownership' above, each succeeding paragraph begins with a phrase that links it to the previous paragraph, in order to maintain continuity of argument:

> *Despite this* (i.e. the lack of a conclusive link)

> *All these claims* (i.e. arguments in favour of home ownership)

5 Practice B

■ Use the information below to write a paragraph about Bill Gates.

1955	Bill Gates was born, the second child in a middle-class Seattle family
1968	At age 13, he became interested in writing computer programmes
1975	Gates and his school friend Allen started a programming business called Microsoft
1980	IBM asked Microsoft to write operating system (called MS-DOS) for its new PC
1985	Microsoft launched Windows operating system
1995	Gates became richest man in world
2006	He stepped down from working at Microsoft to focus on his charitable foundation

SKILLS: USING CONJUNCTIONS

6 Types of conjunctions

Conjunctions are normally found at the start of a sentence, linking back to the sentence before, or in the middle of a sentence, joining the two parts together. There are six main types of conjunctions, each of which help to establish the meaning. Compare:

Demand for food is increasing **because** *the population is growing.*

Mechanisation has increased crop yields, **yet** *production is still inadequate.*

In the first sentence, 'because' introduces a reason, in the second 'yet' indicates a sense of opposition.

■ Underline the conjunctions in the following sentences.

a)   A few inventions, for instance television, have had a major impact on everyday life.

b)   Furthermore, many patients were treated in clinics and surgeries.

c)   The definition of 'special needs' is important since it is the cause of some disagreement.

d)   The technology allows consumers a choice, thus increasing their sense of satisfaction.

e)   Four hundred people were interviewed for the survey, then the results were analysed.

f)   However, another body of opinion associates globalisation with unfavourable outcomes.

■ Match each of the types of conjunction below to one of the sentences above.

i)   Addition   (*b*)

ii)   Result   (   )

iii)   Reason   (   )

iv)   Opposition (   )

v)   Example   (   )

vi)   Time   (   )

7 Practice C

■ Read the paragraph below and underline the conjunctions, then decide what their functions are (i.e. types i–vi above).

BIOFUELS

Newly published research examines some important questions about the growing use of biofuels, <u>such as</u> ethanol made from maize. The production of these has increased sharply recently, but the replacement of food crops with fuel crops has been heavily criticised. Although initially seen as a more environmentally-friendly type of fuel, the research shows that producing some biofuels, for instance biodiesel palm oil, is more polluting than using conventional oil. The ethanol produced from sugar cane, however, can have negative emissions, in other words taking carbon dioxide from the atmosphere instead of adding it. Consequently, it can be seen that the situation is rather confused, and that biofuels are neither a magic solution to the energy problem, nor are they the environmental disaster sometimes suggested.

Conjunction	Type	Conjunction	Type
a) *such as*	*example*	f)	
b)		g)	
c)		h)	
d)		i)	
e)		j)	

8 Common conjunctions

■ Working with a partner, complete the table with as many examples of conjunctions as possible.

Addition	Result	Reason	Opposition	Example	Time

9 Practice D

■ Insert a suitable conjunction into each gap.

a) _____ checking the equipment the experiment was repeated.

b) _____ most people use the train, a minority walk or cycle.

c) Brick is a thermally efficient building material. It is, _____, cheap.

d) Demand has increased for summer courses, _____ extra ones are offered this year.

e) Many writers, _____ Chekhov, have been doctors.

f) _____ the increase in residence fees more students are moving out.

g) _____ Maria was in the lecture her car was being repaired.

h) _____ he was studying Italian he spent a semester in Bologna.

10 Conjunctions of opposition

In some ways, these are the most important type of conjunction, and can be the most difficult to use accurately. Note the position of the conjunctions in the following examples:

The economy is strong, **but/yet** *there are frequent strikes.*

Although/while *there are frequent strikes the economy is strong.*

In spite of/despite *the frequent strikes the economy is strong.*

There are frequent strikes. **However/nevertheless,** *the economy is strong.*

■ Write two sentences in each case.

Example: The equipment was expensive/unreliable.
The equipment was expensive but unreliable.
Although the equipment was expensive it was unreliable.

a)   The government claimed that inflation was falling. The opposition said it was rising.

b)   This department must reduce expenditure. It needs to install new computers.

11 Progress check

■ Use the notes below to write two paragraphs on the subject of 'Trams'. Use conjunctions to organise the paragraphs, and suitable phrases to introduce and link the paragraphs together.

- Trams (streetcars in the USA) were first developed in late nineteenth century

- They provided cheap and convenient mass transport in many cities

- Rail-based systems were expensive to maintain

- Fixed tracks meant that system was inflexible

- During 1950s–60s many European and Asian cities closed tram systems

- Today trams are becoming popular again

- Some cities e.g. Paris, Manchester building new systems

- Trams less polluting than cars and cheaper to operate

- Problems remain with construction costs and traffic congestion blocking tracks

- Expense of building modern tramways means that they remain controversial

Introductions and Conclusions/ Giving Definitions

An effective introduction explains the purpose and scope of the paper to the reader. The conclusion should provide a clear answer to any question asked in the title, as well as summarising the main points. In coursework, both introductions and conclusions are normally written after the main body.

Definitions are usually found in introductions, and attempt to explain what the writer means by a new or specialised term. This unit presents ways of writing both simple and complex definitions.

PROCESS: INTRODUCTIONS AND CONCLUSIONS

1 Introduction contents

Introductions are usually no more than about 10% of the total length of the assignment. Therefore, in a 2,000-word essay, the introduction would be about 200 words. In such a limited space, it is essential to include various specific components.

■ a) What is normally found in an essay introduction? Choose from the list below, and then decide on the best order for the components.

Components	Y/N
i) A definition of any unfamiliar terms in the title	
ii) Your opinions on the subject of the essay	
iii) An outline of the main body of the essay	

Components	Y/N
iv) A provocative idea or question to interest the reader	
v) Your aim or purpose in writing	
vi) The method you adopt to answer the question	
vii) Some brief background to the topic	
viii) Any limitations you set yourself	
ix) Mention of some sources you have read on the topic	

■ b) Read the extracts below from introductions to articles and decide which of the components listed above (i–ix) they are examples of.

A) In the past twenty years the ability of trial juries to assess complex or lengthy cases has been widely debated.

B) The rest of the paper is organised as follows. The second section explains why corporate governance is important for economic prosperity. The third section presents the model specification and describes the data and variables used in our empirical analysis. The fourth section reports and discusses the empirical results. The fifth section concludes.

C) The purpose of this paper is to investigate changes in the incidence of extreme warm and cold temperatures over the globe since 1870.

D) There is no clear empirical evidence sustaining a 'managerial myopia' argument. Pugh *et al.* (1992) find evidence that supports such a theory, but Meulbrook *et al.* (1990), Mahoney *et al.* (1997), Garvey and Hanka (1999) and a study by the Office of the Chief Economist of the Securities and Exchange Commission (1985) find no evidence.

E) 'Social cohesion' is usually defined in reference to common aims and objectives, social order, social solidarity and the sense of place attachment.

F) This study will focus on mergers in the media business between 1995 and 2010, since with more recent examples an accurate assessment of the consequences cannot yet be made.

2 Introduction structure

There is no standard pattern for an introduction, since much depends on the type of research you are conducting and the length of your work, but this is a common structure:

a   Definition of key terms, if needed

b   Relevant background information

c   Review of work by other writers on the topic

d   Purpose or aim of the paper

e   Your research methods

f   Any limitations you imposed

g   An outline of your paper

■ **Study the extracts below from the introduction to an essay titled: 'Evaluate the experience of e-learning for students in higher education.'**

a)   Certain words or phrases in the title may need clarifying because they are not widely understood:

There is a range of definitions of this term, but in this paper 'e-learning' refers to any type of learning situation where content is delivered via the internet.

b)   It is useful to remind the reader of the wider context of your work. This may also show the value of the study you have carried out:

Learning is one of the most vital components of the contemporary knowledge-based economy. With the development of computing power and technology the internet has become an essential medium for knowledge transfer.

c)   While a longer article may have a separate literature review, in a shorter essay it is still important to show familiarity with researchers who have studied this topic previously. This may also reveal a gap in research that justifies your work:

Various researchers (Webb and Kirstin, 2003; Honig et al., 2006) have evaluated e-learning in a healthcare and business context, but little attention so far has been paid to the reactions of students in higher education to this method of teaching.

d)   The aim of your research must be clearly stated so the reader knows what you are trying to do:

The purpose of this study was to examine students' experience of e-learning in a higher education context.

e)   The method demonstrates the process that you undertook to achieve the aim given before:

A range of studies was first reviewed, and then a survey of 200 students was conducted to assess their experience of e-learning.

f)   You cannot deal with every aspect of this topic in an essay, so you must make clear the boundaries of your study:

Clearly a study of this type is inevitably restricted by various constraints, notably the size of the student sample, and this was limited to students of Pharmacy and Agriculture.

g)   Understanding the structure of your work will help the reader to follow your argument:

The paper is structured as follows. The first section presents an analysis of the relevant research, focusing on the current limited knowledge regarding the student experience. The second part presents the methodology of the survey and an analysis of the findings, and the final section considers the implications of the results for the delivery of e-learning programmes.

The complete introduction is as follows:

EVALUATE THE EXPERIENCE OF E-LEARNING FOR STUDENTS IN HIGHER EDUCATION

There is a range of definitions of this term, but in this paper 'e-learning' refers to any type of learning situation where content is delivered via the internet. Learning is one of the most vital components of the contemporary knowledge-based economy. With the development of computing power and technology the internet has become an essential medium for knowledge transfer. Various researchers (Webb and Kirstin, 2003; Honig et al., 2006) have evaluated e-learning in a healthcare and business context, but little attention so far has been paid to the reactions of students in higher education (HE) to this method of teaching. The purpose of this study was to examine students' experience of e-learning in an HE context.

A range of studies was first reviewed, and then a survey of 200 students was conducted to assess their experience of e-learning. Clearly a study of this type is inevitably restricted by various constraints, notably the size of the student sample, and this was limited to students of Pharmacy and Agriculture. The paper is structured as follows. The first section presents an analysis of the relevant research, focusing on the current limited knowledge regarding the student experience. The second part presents the methodology of the survey and an analysis of the findings, and the final section considers the implications of the results for the delivery of e-learning programmes.

(224 words)

3 Opening sentences

It can be difficult to start writing an essay, but especially in exams, hesitation will waste valuable time. The first few sentences should be general but not vague, to help the reader focus on the topic. They often have the following pattern:

Time phrase	Topic	Development
Currently,	the control of water resources	has emerged as potential cause of international friction.
Since 2012	electric vehicles	have become a serious commercial proposition.

It is important to avoid opening sentences that are over-general and vague. Compare:

Nowadays there is a lot of competition among different news providers.   ✗

Newspapers are currently facing strong competition from rival news providers such as the internet and television.   ✓

■ **Write introductory sentences for two of the following titles.**

a)   **Are there any technological solutions to global warming?**

b)   What can be done to reduce infant mortality in developing countries?

c)   Compare the urbanisation process in two contrasting countries.

4 Conclusions

Conclusions tend to be shorter and more varied in format than introductions. Some articles may have a 'summary' or 'concluding remarks'. But student papers should generally have a final section that summarises the arguments and makes it clear to the reader that the original question has been answered.

■ **Which of the following are generally acceptable in conclusions?**

a)   A statement showing how your aim has been achieved.

b)   A discussion of the implications of your research.

c)   Some new information on the topic not mentioned before.

d)   A short review of the main results of your study.

e)   Some suggestions for further research.

f)   The limitations of your study.

g)   Comparison with the results of similar studies.

h)   A quotation that appears to sum up your work.

■ **Match the extracts from conclusions below with the acceptable components above. Example: a = vi**

i)   As always, this investigation has a number of limitations to be considered in evaluating its findings.

ii)   These results suggest that the risk of flooding on this coast has increased significantly and is likely to worsen.

iii)   Another line of research worth pursuing further is to study the importance of language for successful expatriate assignments.

iv)   Our review of 13 studies of strikes in public transport demonstrates that the effect of a strike on public transport ridership varies and may either be temporary or permanent.

v)   These results of the Colombia study reported here are consistent with other similar studies conducted in other countries (Baron and Norman, 1992).

vi) This study has clearly illustrated the drawbacks to family ownership of retail businesses.

5 Practice A

■ The following sentences form the conclusion to the essay titled 'Evaluate the experience of e-learning for students in higher education', whose introduction was given in 2 above, but they have been mixed up. Put them into a logical order (1–5).

i)   This finding was clear, despite the agreed convenience of e-learning.

ii) Given the constraints of the small and limited sample there is clearly room for further research in this field.

iii) However, our survey of nearly 200 students found a strong preference for traditional classroom teaching.

iv) But in general it would appear that e-learning is unlikely to be acceptable as a primary teaching method in Higher Education.

v)   This study found that little relevant research on the HE student experience of e-learning has been conducted, and the research that has been reported indicates a mixed reaction to it.

SKILLS: GIVING DEFINITIONS

6 Simple definitions

Definitions are not needed in every essay introduction, but if the title includes an unfamiliar phrase, or if the writer wants to use a term in a special way, it is important to make clear to the reader exactly what is meant in this context. Basic definitions are formed by giving a category and the application:

Word	Category	Application
An agenda	is a set of issues	to be discussed in a meeting.
A Master's degree	is an academic award	for postgraduate students, given on successful completion of coursework and a dissertation.
A grant	is a sum of money	given for a specific purpose.
A seminar	is an academic class	meeting with a tutor for study.

■ Complete the following definitions by inserting a suitable category word or phrase from the box (there are more words than gaps).

> material   theory   behaviour   organisation   organs
> instrument   process   period   grains   profession

a) A barometer is a scientific _____ designed to measure atmospheric pressure.

b) Kidneys are _____ that separate waste fluid from the blood.

c) A multi-national company is a business _____ that operates in many countries.

d) Reinforced concrete is a building _____ consisting of cement, sand, aggregate and steel rods.

e) Bullying is a pattern of anti-social _____ found in many schools.

f) Recycling is a _____ in which materials are used again.

g) A recession is a _____ of reduced economic activity.

h) Cereals are _____ widely grown for food production.

■ Write definitions for the following:

i) A lecture is _____.

j) An idiom is _____.

■ Write two definitions from your own subject area.

7 Complex definitions

■ Study the following examples and underline the terms being defined.

a) The definition for a failed project ranges from abandoned projects to projects that do not meet their full potential or simply have schedule overrun problems.

b)   Development is a socio-economic-technological process having the main objective of raising the standards of living of the people.

c)   Bowlby (1982) suggested that attachment is an organised system whose goal is to make individuals feel safe and secure.

d)   Globalisation, in an economic sense, describes the opening up of national economies to global markets and global capital, the freer movement and diffusion of goods, services, finance, people, knowledge and technology around the world.

These examples illustrate the variety of methods used in giving definitions.

■ **Which of the above example(s)**

i)   quotes a definition from another writer?

ii)   gives a variety of relevant situations?

iii) explains a process?

8 Progress check

When writing introductions, it is often useful to define a term in the title, even if it is fairly common, in order to demonstrate your understanding of its meaning.

Example:

Title: 'Higher education should be free and open to all – discuss.'

Definition: *Higher education usually means university-level study for first or higher degrees, normally at the age of 18 or above.*

■ **Study the following titles, underline the terms that are worth defining and write definitions for three of them.**

a)   Capital punishment has no place in the modern legal system – discuss.

b)   How can the management of an entrepreneurial business retain its entrepreneurial culture as it matures?

c)   E-books are likely to replace printed books in the next twenty years. Do you agree?

d) As urban areas continue to expand worldwide, will agriculture be able to feed the growing population of cities?

e) Given the medical dangers of obesity, what is the best way of reducing its incidence?

Rewriting and Proofreading/ Academic Style

In exams, you have no time for rewriting, but for coursework it is important to take time to revise your work to improve its clarity and logical development. In both situations, proofreading is essential to avoid the small errors that may make parts of your work inaccurate or difficult to understand.

There is no one correct style of academic writing, but in general it should attempt to be accurate, impersonal and objective. This unit gives guidelines for an appropriate style, and provides practice.

PROCESS: REWRITING AND PROOFREADING

1 Rewriting

Although it is tempting to think that the first draft of an essay is good enough, it almost certainly can be improved. After completing your first draft, you should leave it for a day and then reread it, asking yourself the following questions:

a) Does this fully answer the question(s) in the title?

b) Is there the right balance between different sections of the paper?

c) Does the argument or discussion develop clearly and logically?

d) Have I forgotten any important points that would support the development?

As part of a module on Qualitative Research Methods, you have written the first draft of a 1,000-word paper titled: 'What would be an acceptable number of interviews to carry out for a Master's dissertation?'

■ Study the introduction to this paper below, and decide how it could be improved, listing your suggestions in the table.

An interview can be defined as a conversation with a definite structure and objective. It goes beyond an everyday discussion with no particular purpose. There are many possible interview situations, but all involve an interviewer and an interviewee. It is normal for the former to ask the latter direct questions, and record the answers. The questions may be prepared in advance or they may occur as the interview develops. The recording is often done on paper, but may also be done by audio or video recording. Interviews can take place anywhere, in a street, café, office, bar, restaurant etc. It is hard to say how many interviews can be carried out in one day. I personally think that two is the maximum because it can get very tiring. A lot depends on the subject being researched.

	Suggestions for improvement
a)	
b)	
c)	
d)	
e)	

Comments on the first draft might include the following:

a)   Too much space given to basic points

b)   No sources are mentioned

c)   Sentences are too short

d)   Style e.g. *I personally think* not suitable

e)   Question in title not fully addressed

With these points in mind, the introduction could be rewritten as follows:

Organising an interview involves a series of steps (Davies, 2007) including recruiting interviewees, finding a suitable venue and writing appropriate guidelines. However, depending on the research subject a more flexible approach can be adopted, resulting in a less structured interview (Cooper and Schindler, 2008). For a Master's dissertation, interviews must contain data relevant to the research topic which the interviewer can later process. As King states: 'gathering a large volume of cases does not guarantee the credibility of a study' (King, 2004:16). Most writers agree that two one-hour interviews per day are effectively the maximum for one interviewer, given the time needed for preparation and subsequent processing. Moreover, if audio or video recording is used there is more content to be analysed, for instance in terms of facial expression. The analysis of one interview can take up to three days' work. In order to answer the question, clearly much depends on the research topic and the time the researcher has available.

2 Practice A

■ **Read the next section on 'Possible ethical issues raised by this kind of research'. Decide how it could be improved, and rewrite it.**

Any organisation that allows researchers to interview its employees runs a big risk. The interviewees may complain about the boss or about other workers. Another danger for the researcher is that employees may feel obliged to give positive answers to questions instead of their honest opinions, because they are afraid of their bosses finding out what they really think. Also the reputation of the organisation may suffer. I believe that researchers should make sure that this does not happen. They must make it clear why they are doing the research, and keep everyone's name secret by using false names. If this is not done there's a good chance that the validity of the whole research project will be threatened.

3 Proofreading

a) Proofreading means checking your work for small errors that may make it more difficult for the reader to understand exactly what you want to say. If a sentence has only one error:

She has no enough interpersonal skills to handle different relationships.

it is not difficult to understand, but if there are multiple errors, even though they are all quite minor, the effect is very confusing:

A american senate once say: 'Truth is frist casualty off war'.

Clearly, you should aim to make your meaning as clear as possible. Note that computer spellchecks do not always help you, since they may ignore a word that is spelt correctly but which is not the word you meant to use:

Tow factors need to be considered . . .

■ Examples of the most common types of error in student writing are shown below. In each case, underline the error and correct it.

i)   **Factual:** *corruption is a problem in many countries such as Africa*

ii) **Word ending:** *she was young and innocence*

iii) **Punctuation:** *What is the optimum size for a research team*

iv) **Tense:** *Since 2005 there were three major earthquakes in the region*

v)   **Vocabulary:** *. . . vital to the successfulness of a company operating in China*

vi) **Spelling:** *pervious experience can sometimes give researchers . . .*

vii) **Singular/plural:** *one of the largest company in Asia*

viii) **Style:** *. . . finally, the essay will conclude with a conclusion*

ix) **Missing word:** *an idea established by David Ricardo in nineteenth century*

x)   **Word order:** *a rule of marketing which states that consumers when go out shopping . . .*

4 Practice B

■ Underline the errors in the paragraph below and correct them.

Bicycle is one of most efficient machine ever designed. Cyclists can travel for times faster than walkers; when using less enorgy to do so. Various people invented early versions of the bicycle, but the first modle with pedals which was successful mass-produced was make by a frenchman, Ernest Michaux, on 1861. Later aditions included pneumatic tyres and gears. Today hundreds of million of bicycles are in use over all world.

SKILLS: ACADEMIC STYLE

5 Components of academic style

There are few fixed rules for academic style that apply to all disciplines, so students should study examples of writing in their own subject area, and then aim to develop their own 'voice'. But certain general guidelines apply in most cases.

■ Study this paragraph and underline any examples of poor style.

> How to make people work harder is a topic that lots of people have written about in the last few years. There are lots of different theories etc and I think some of them are ok. When we think about this we should remember the old Chinese proverb, that you can lead a horse to water but you can't make it drink. So how do we increase production? It's quite a complex subject but I'll just talk about a couple of ideas.

Some of the problems with the style of this paragraph can be analysed as follows:

Poor style	Reason
How to make people work harder . . .	Imprecise vocabulary – use 'motivation'
. . . lots of people . . .	Vague – give names
. . . the last few years.	Vague – give dates
lots of different . . .	Avoid 'lots of'
. . . etc . . .	Avoid using 'etc' and 'so on'
. . . I think . . .	Too personal
. . . are ok.	Too informal
When we think about this . . .	Too personal
. . . the old Chinese proverb . . .	Do not quote proverbs or similar expressions
So how do we increase production?	Avoid rhetorical questions
It's quite a . . .	Avoid contractions
. . . I'll just talk about a couple . . .	Too personal and informal

The paragraph could be rewritten in more suitable style:

> Motivation has been the subject of numerous studies in the last 60 years, but this essay will focus on Maslow's hierarchy of needs theory (1943) and Herzberg's two-factor theory (1966). Their contemporary relevance to the need to motivate employees effectively will be examined critically, given that this can be considered crucial to a firm's survival in the current economic climate.

6 Guidelines

a) Do not use idiomatic or colloquial vocabulary: *kids*, *boss*. Instead, use standard English: *children*, *manager*.

b) Use vocabulary accurately. There is a difference between *rule* and *law*, or *weather* and *climate*, which you are expected to know if you study these subjects.

c) Be as precise as possible when dealing with facts or figures. Avoid phrases such as *about a hundred* or *hundreds of years ago*. If it is necessary to estimate numbers, use *approximately* rather than *about*.

d) Conclusions should use tentative language. Avoid absolute statements such as *unemployment causes crime*. Instead use cautious phrases: *unemployment may cause crime* or *tends to cause crime*.

e) Avoid adverbs that show your personal attitude: *luckily*, *remarkably*, *surprisingly*.

f) Do not contract verb forms: *don't*, *can't*. Use the full form: *do not*, *cannot*.

g) Although academic English tends to use the passive more than standard English, it should not be overused. Both are needed. Compare:

> *Galileo discovered the moons of Jupiter.*

> *The moons of Jupiter were discovered by Galileo.*

In the first case, the focus is on Galileo, in the second (passive) on the moons.

h) Avoid the following:

- *like* for introducing examples. Use *such as* or *for instance.*

- *thing* and combinations *nothing* or *something*. Use *factor, issue* or *topic*.

- *lots of*. Use *a significant/considerable number.*

- *little/big*. Use *small/large.*

- • 'get' phrases such as *get better/worse.* Use *improve* and *deteriorate.*

- • *good/bad* are simplistic. Use *positive/negative* (e.g. *the changes had several positive aspects*)

i) Do not use question forms such as *Why did war break out in 1914?* Instead, use statements: *There were three reasons for the outbreak of war . . .*

j) Avoid numbering sections of your text, except in reports and long essays. Use conjunctions and signposting expressions to introduce new sections (*Turning to the question of detecting cancer . . .*).

k) When writing lists, avoid using *etc.* or *and so on.* Insert *and* before the last item:

   > *The main products were pharmaceuticals, electronic goods and confectionery.*

l) Avoid using two-word verbs such as *go on* or *bring up* if there is a suitable synonym. Use *continue* or *raise.*

7 Practice C

■ In the following sentences, underline examples of bad style and rewrite them in a more suitable way.

a) Another thing to think about is the chance of crime getting worse.

b) Regrettably these days lots of people don't have jobs.

c) Sometime soon they will find a vaccine for malaria.

d) A few years ago the price of property in Japan went down a lot.

e) You can't always trust the numbers in that report.

f) Sadly, the high inflation led to poverty, social unrest and so on.

g) He was over the moon when he won the prize.

h) I think we should pay students to study.

i) A few years ago they allowed women to vote.

j) What were the main causes of the Russian revolution?

8 Varying sentence length

Short sentences are clear and easy to read:

> *Car scrappage schemes have been introduced in many countries.*

But too many short sentences are monotonous:

> *Car scrappage schemes have been introduced in many countries. They offer a subsidy to buyers of new cars. The buyers must scrap an old vehicle. The schemes are designed to stimulate the economy. They also increase fuel efficiency.*

Long sentences are more interesting but can be difficult to construct and read:

> *Car scrappage schemes, which offer a subsidy to buyers of new cars (who must scrap an old vehicle) have been introduced in many countries; the schemes are designed to stimulate the economy and also increase fuel efficiency.*

Effective writing normally uses a mixture of long and short sentences, often using a short sentence to introduce the topic:

> *Car scrappage schemes have been introduced in many countries. They offer a subsidy to buyers of new cars, who must scrap an old vehicle. The schemes are designed to stimulate the economy and also increase fuel efficiency.*

■ **Rewrite the following paragraph so that instead of six short sentences, there are two long and two short sentences.**

Worldwide, enrolments in higher education are increasing. In developed countries over half of all young people enter college. Similar trends are seen in China and South America. This growth has put financial strain on state university systems. Many countries are asking students and parents to contribute financially. This leads to a debate about whether students or society benefit from tertiary education.

Until you feel confident in your writing, it is better to use shorter rather than longer sentences. This should make your meaning as clear as possible.

9 The use of caution

A cautious style is necessary in many areas of academic writing to avoid making statements that can be contradicted:

> *Crime is linked to poor education.*

Such statements are rarely completely true. There is usually an exception that needs to be considered. Caution can be shown in several ways:

*Crime **may** be linked to poor education.*   (modal verb)

*Crime is **frequently** linked to poor education.*   (adverb)

*Crime **tends to** be linked to poor education.*   (verb)

Areas where caution is particularly important include:

a)   outlining a hypothesis that needs to be tested (e.g. in an introduction)

b)   discussing the results of a study, which may not be conclusive

c)   commenting on the work of other writers

d)   making predictions (normally with **may** or **might**)

■ Complete the table below with more examples of each.

Modals	Adverbs	Verb/phrase
can	*commonly*	*tends to*

10 Using modifiers

Another way to express caution is to use **quite**, **rather** or **fairly** before an adjective:

NB: **quite** is often used before the article. It is generally used positively, while **rather** tends to be used negatively:

*a **fairly** accurate summary*

*a **rather** inconvenient location*

***quite** a significant discovery*

■ Insert quite/rather/fairly in the following to emphasise caution.

a)   The company's efforts to save energy were successful.

b)   The survey was a comprehensive study of student opinion.

c)   His second book had a hostile reception.

d)   The first year students were fascinated by her lectures.

e)   The latest type of arthritis drug is expensive.

11 Progress check

■ Rewrite the following paragraph in a more academic style.

Everybody needs energy, but nobody can agree on a good way to get it. Getting energy from coal is cheap, but burning coal is dirty. Using gas is also cheap, but still makes carbon dioxide. Some people think nuclear power is best, because it doesn't add to global warming. Sadly, nuclear power stations cost a lot to build and can blow up. So what's left? Wind or solar power are other options. These are renewable sources, because they don't get used up. The snag is that the wind doesn't blow everyday and the sun doesn't shine at night. So it looks like there are no easy answers.

Elements of Writing

Academic Vocabulary
Nouns and Adjectives

International students may be understandably concerned by the amount of vocabulary required for reading academic texts in their subject area. But developing vocabulary involves more than learning lists of words: it is helpful to think first about word class. This unit focuses on nouns and adjectives; Unit 2.2 looks at verbs and adverbs.

1 Introduction

To read and write academic papers effectively, students need to be familiar with the rather formal vocabulary that is widely used. But it is worth remembering that much of that vocabulary is specific to your subject area, for example in the sentence:

The effectiveness of this malaria vaccine has been a subject of controversy.

'malaria vaccine' will be understood by medical students, while 'effectiveness' and 'controversy' are general academic vocabulary that all students need to understand. The focus of this course is on the general vocabulary common to most disciplines.

2 Nouns

■ Study the following table of common nouns, with examples of use. With a partner, discuss the meaning of each noun.

accuracy	Repeating the experiment will improve the **accuracy** of the results.
analysis	His **analysis** of the alloy showed a high percentage of copper.
approach	Professor Han has brought a new **approach** to the study of genetics.

assessment	*She failed the first module **assessment** but passed the final one.*
assumption	*He made the **assumption** that all the students spoke French.*
authority	*Dr James is our leading **authority** on marine law.*
category	*Her work established two **categories** of local governance.*
claim	*Their **claim** that the island was first inhabited in 550 BCE is false.*
controversy	*Climate change is an issue that has caused much **controversy**.*
correlation	*They found a **correlation** between height and health.*
deterrent	*The harsh climate of the desert acted as a **deterrent** to exploration.*
emphasis	*Their teacher put the **emphasis** on practical research.*
evidence	*The X-ray provided **evidence** of his lung infection.*
exception	*The Tesla is an **exception** to the idea of slow, small electric cars.*
extract	*He read a short **extract** from his paper on Hegel to the class.*
ideology	*Military power was at the heart of Roman **ideology**.*
implication	*The **implication** of the report is that we need to do more research.*
innovation	*Steam power was a significant **innovation** in the eighteenth century*
intuition	***Intuition** has been described as 'a gut feeling'.*
motivation	*Money is often claimed to be the **motivation** for most workers.*
perspective	*Sigmund Freud's work opened a new **perspective** on human behaviour.*
phenomenon	*Earthquakes are an unusual **phenomenon** in Britain.*
policy	*The university has a zero-tolerance **policy** on plagiarism.*
preference	*Her **preference** was criminal law, but other fields were more profitable.*
process	*The drug trials involved a three-stage **process** that took two years.*
proposal	*The professor's **proposal** for more seminars was rejected.*
provision	*The library has increased its **provision** of computer terminals by 100%.*
sequence	*Writing is a **sequence** of reading, note-taking, planning and drafting.*
strategy	*Swimming every day was part of his **strategy** for getting fit.*
substitute	*To what extent can natural gas be a **substitute** for oil?*
technique	*She developed a new **technique** for collecting the beetles.*
validity	*Events confirmed the **validity** of his prediction.*

■ **Complete each sentence with a suitable noun.**

a) The excavation found no _____ of human settlement
   before 1250 BCE.

b) The tutor asked the class for their _____ for next
   semester's topics.

c) Many great discoveries were based on _____ rather than
   logic.

d) Due to the rising birth rate _____ was made for more
   school places.

e) Few believed Galileo's _____ that the earth went round
   the sun.

3 Using nouns and adjectives

It is easy to confuse the noun and adjective form of words such as 'possible'
and 'possibility'.

■ **Compare these sentences:**

*The **efficiency** of the machine depends on the **precision** of its construction.*

***Precise** construction results in an **efficient** machine.*

The first sentence uses the nouns 'efficiency' and 'precision'. The second uses
adjectives: 'precise' and 'efficient'. Although the meaning is similar, the first
sentence is more formal. Effective academic writing requires accurate use of
both nouns and adjectives.

■ **Complete the gaps in the table below.**

Noun	Adjective	Noun	Adjective
approximation	approximate		particular
superiority		reason	
	strategic		synthetic
politics		economic/economy	

Noun	Adjective	Noun	Adjective
	industrial		cultural
exterior		average	
	high		reliable
heat		strength	
	confident		true
width		probability	
	necessary		long
danger		relevance	

4 Practice A

■ Insert a suitable noun or adjective from the table into each sentence.

a) The students were _____ their project would be successful.

b) One of Tokyo's _____ is its excellent transport system.

c) There is a strong _____ that fees will rise next year.

d) The students complained that the lecture was not _____ to their course.

e) The results are so surprising it will be _____ to repeat the experiment.

f) Regularly backing up computer files reduces the _____ of losing vital work.

g) Revising for exams is a tedious _____.

h) The _____ date of the founding of Rome is 750 BCE.

i) The _____ consequences of the war were inflation and unemployment.

j) They attempted to make a _____ of all the different proposals.

5 Academic adjectives

The following adjectives are best understood and learnt as opposites:

absolute	relative
abstract	concrete
accurate	inaccurate
ambiguous	unambiguous
analytic	synthetic
effective	ineffective
exclusive	inclusive
logical	illogical
metaphorical	literal
precise	vague or approximate or rough
rational	irrational
reliable	unreliable
relevant	irrelevant
specific	non-specific
subjective	objective
theoretical	practical or empirical or pragmatic

*Inflation is an **abstract** concept.*

*The **metaphorical** use of the word 'key' is probably more common than its **literal** one.*

*The study of engineering is very **relevant** to architecture.*

*Her study of women in education was criticised for being too **subjective**.*

*In Europe, **empirical** research began in the sixteenth century.*

■ **Find related nouns for as many of the words in the left-hand column as possible.**

6 Practice B

■ Underline the adjective in each sentence and write the related noun in brackets.

Example:
Several steel producers are <u>likely</u> to shut down next year. (*likelihood*)

a) The HR team have just completed a strategic review of pay.
    (_____)

b) Dr Lee adopted an analytical approach to the inquiry. (_____)

c) Nylon was one of the earliest synthetic fibres. (_____)

d) Her major contribution to the research was her study of ante-natal care. (_____)

e) All advertising must respect cultural differences. (_____)

f) Some progress was made in the theoretical area. (_____)

g) A frequent complaint is that too much reading is expected.
    (_____)

h) We took a more critical approach to marketing theory. (_____)

i) The Department of Social Policy is offering three courses this year.
    (_____)

j) Finally, the practical implications of my findings will be examined.
    (_____)

Students wishing to develop their academic vocabulary should study the Academic Word List (AWL). This is a list of 570 items commonly found in academic texts across various disciplines, created by Averil Coxhead.

See Sandra Haywood's website for information about the AWL, with further practice exercises: www.nottingham.ac.uk/~alzsh3/acvocab/

Academic Vocabulary

Verbs and Adverbs

> When reading a text, it is useful to identify and understand the main verbs: this is often the key to understanding the whole sentence. This unit examines some of the more formal verbs used in academic writing, and outlines the use of adverbs.

1 Understanding main verbs

■ Study the following sentence and underline the main verbs:

> The author concludes that no reasonable alternative is currently available to replace constitutional democracy, even though he does not completely reject the possibility of creating a better political system in the future.

To follow the writer's meaning, the reader needs to be clear that 'concludes' and 'reject' are the main verbs in the two parts of the sentence. Academic writing tends to use rather formal verbs to express the writer's meaning accurately:

*In the last decade the pace of change has **accelerated**.*

*Could Darwin have **envisaged** the controversy his work has caused?*

In spoken English, we are more likely to use 'speed up' and 'imagined'.

■ Study the list below and find a synonym in each case.

Verb	Example of use	Synonym
to adapt	the health system has been **adapted** from France	*modified*
to arise	a similar situation **arises** when we look at younger children	
to conduct	the largest study was **conducted** in Finland	
to characterise	developing countries are **characterised** by . . .	
to clarify	the project was designed to **clarify** these contradictions	
to concentrate on	that study **concentrated on** older children	
to be concerned with	the programme is **concerned** primarily **with** . . .	
to demonstrate	further research has **demonstrated** that few factors . . .	
to determine	the water content was experimentally **determined**	
to discriminate	a failure to **discriminate** between two species	
to establish	the northern boundary was **established** first	
to exhibit	half of the patients **exhibited** signs of improvement	
to focus on	her work **focused on** female managers	
to generate	a question which has **generated** a range of responses	
to hold	Newton's second law, $F = ma$, **holds** everywhere	
to identify	three main areas have been **identified**	
to imply	his absence **implies** a lack of interest	
to interact	understand how the two systems **interact**	
to interpret	the result can be **interpreted** as a limited success	
to manifest	as **manifested** in anti-social behaviour	
to overcome	both difficulties were **overcome** in the first week	
to propose	they **propose** that social class is the main factor	
to prove	the use of solar power is **proving** successful	

Verb	Example of use	Synonym
to recognise	he is now **recognised** as a leading expert	
to relate to	the pattern was **related to** both social and physical factors	
to supplement	the diet was **supplemented** with calcium and iodine	
to undergo	the system **underwent** major changes in the 1980s	
to yield	both surveys **yielded** mixed results	

(Some of these verbs, e.g. 'hold', are used in academic work with a special meaning).

2 Practice A

■ Complete the following sentences using verbs from the list above.

a) He _____ repeating the experiment to confirm the result.

b) Two main problems _____ when the medical team began the vaccination programme.

c) When the students looked puzzled she tried to _____ her explanation.

d) The methods used successfully in Spain were _____ for the cooler climate in Norway.

e) His new book _____ on the literature of the nineteenth century.

f) They _____ drinking water as the source of infection.

g) Most of his research was _____ in the slums of Sao Paulo.

h) The study clearly _____ that older employees are more reliable.

3 Using adverbs

In the sentence given in section 1, adverbs are used to give information about time (currently) and degree (completely):

> *The author concludes that no reasonable alternative is **currently** available to replace constitutional democracy, even though he does not **completely** reject the possibility of creating a better political system in the future.*

Adverbs are used in academic writing in a variety of ways. Among the most important are:

a)   to provide more detail, with verbs and adjectives:

> ***Reasonably** good data are only available for the last two centuries.*

> *Decomposition **eventually** ceases in modern landfills.*

b)   individually, often at the beginning of sentences, to introduce new points or link sentences together:

> ***Currently**, the Earth's atmosphere appears to be warming up.*

> ***Alternatively**, the use of non-conventional renewable energies is increasing.*

NB: Adverbs used individually need to be employed with care. It is dangerous to overuse them, since they are often like the author's 'voice', commenting on the topic. As the academic writer aims to be objective, adverbs such as 'fortunately' or 'remarkably' may be unsuitable.

Adverbs linked to verbs and adjectives usually fall into three groups.

i)   Time (when?)

> ***previously** published*

> ***retrospectively** examined*

ii)   Degree (how much?)

> *declined **considerably***

> *contribute **substantially***

iii)   Manner (in what way?)

> ***medically** complicated*

> ***remotely** located*

Further common examples include:

Time	Degree	Manner
recently	*particularly*	*factually*
increasingly	*broadly*	*politically*
originally	*highly*	*locally*
currently	*wholly*	*alternatively*
traditionally	*crucially*	*similarly*
continuously	*emphatically*	*psychologically*

4 Practice B

■ **Insert a suitable adverb from the table above into the gaps in the sentences.**

a) She was _____ affected by the trauma of the accident.

b) _____, the internet was mainly used for academic purposes.

c) Some courses are assessed purely by exams. _____, coursework may be employed.

d) _____, there has been growing concern about financing the health service.

e) Many birds use bright colours to attract a mate. _____, flowers advertise their position to fertilising insects.

f) _____, their houses were built of mud and straw.

Making Comparisons

It is often necessary to make comparisons in academic writing. The comparison might be the subject of the essay, or might provide evidence for the argument. In all cases, it is important to explain clearly what is being compared and to make the comparison as accurate as possible. This unit deals with different forms of comparison and practises their use.

1 Comparison structures

a) Some studies are based on a comparison:

The purpose of this study is to compare Chinese and American consumers on their propensity to use self-service technology in a retail setting.

In other cases, a comparison provides useful context:

The first attempt to decode the human genome took 10 years; now it can be done in less than a week.

b) The two basic comparative forms are:

i)   *France is **larger** than Switzerland.*

*The students were **happier** after the exam.*

(-er is added to one-syllable adjectives and two-syllable adjectives ending in -y, which changes into an 'i')

ii) *Learning Chinese is **more difficult** than learning English.*

(more . . . is used with other adjectives of two or more syllables)

Compare these three structures:

Parisian property is more expensive than Roman (property).

Property in Paris is more expensive than in Rome.

The price of property in Paris is higher than in Rome.

c) These comparisons can be modified by the use of adverbs such as *slightly, marginally, approximately, considerably, significantly* and *substantially.*

*France is **substantially larger** than Switzerland.*

*Switzerland is **slightly smaller** than Holland.*

*Winters in Poland are **significantly colder** than in Portugal.*

d) Similarity can be noted by the use of *as . . . as* or *the same as*:

*The population of France is approximately **the same as** the population of Britain.*

*Summers in Tokyo are **as wet as** in Singapore.*

This form can be used for quantitative comparison:

*Britain is **half as large as** France.* (also *twice as large as, ten times as fast as*)

e) Note that high/low are used for comparing abstract ideas (e.g. rates):

*The birth rate was **higher** 20 years ago.*

more/less must be used with *than + comparison*:

*This module is **more difficult than** the last one.*

*Divorce is **less common** in Turkey **than** in Germany.*

■ **Write four sentences comparing your country with another you know well.**

2 Using superlatives (e.g. the largest/smallest)

When using superlatives, take care to define the group (e.g. 'the cheapest car' has no meaning):

*The cheapest car **in the Ford range/in the USA**.*

the most/the least are followed by an adjective:

*The **most interesting** example is Ireland . . .*

the most/the fewest are used in relation to numbers:

> **The fewest** *students studied biogenetics (i.e. the lowest number)*

3 Practice A

■ Study the table, which shows the income of the top ten clubs in European football. Then read the comparisons. Each sentence contains one error. Find and correct it.

Income of leading European football clubs 2012–13

Club	Revenue €m.
Real Madrid	518
FC Barcelona	482
Bayern Munich	431
Manchester United	423
Paris Saint Germain	398
Manchester City	316
Chelsea	303
Arsenal	284
Juventus	272
AC Milan	263

a)   Real Madrid was the richest football club.

b)   Real Madrid's income was almost twice much as AC Milan's.

c)   FC Barcelona earned marginally more than Manchester City.

d)   Juventus had less revenue Arsenal.

e)   Chelsea's income was slightly lower than Bayern Munich's.

f)   Manchester United earned approximately same as Bayern Munich.

4 Practice B

■ Study the table below and complete the gaps in the paragraph (one word per gap).

Marriage and divorce rates (per 1,000 population) (Source: UN)

Country	Marriage rate	Divorce rate
Egypt	10.6	1.5
United States	8.4	4.7
Iran	8.4	0.8
Turkey	8.3	0.6
Japan	6.2	1.9
Russia	5.2	2.9
Spain	5.2	0.8
United Kingdom	5.2	3.1
South Africa	4.0	0.9
Libya	3.9	0.3

The table a) _____ marriage and divorce rates in a variety of countries. The marriage b) _____ ranges from 10.6 per thousand in Egypt to 3.9 in Libya, while the rate of divorce c) _____ even more, from 4.7 in the USA to only 0.3 in Libya. The marriage rate in America is the d) _____ as in Iran, which has a e) _____ higher rate f) _____ Turkey's. In countries such as Iran, Turkey and Libya only 10% of marriages appear to end in divorce, but in Russia and the USA the number is g) _____ half. It seems possible that the h) _____ marriage rate in the USA may be partly due to second marriages.

5 Practice C

■ Study the data below about London. Then use some of it to write a comparison with a city you know well.

Location: on River Thames, not far from coast – was a major port

History: a town has been on this site for about 2,000 years

Status: national capital

Population: over 7 million

Employment: Government offices, banking, finance, retail, entertainment

Culture: 240 museums, 100 theatres

Public transport: London had the world's first underground railway, the 'Tube'. This now has 275 stations on 12 lines. Plus red double-decker buses and black taxis

Climate: Cool wet winters, warm wet summers. Summer average approximately 17 °C.

Housing: Mainly brick terraced houses, some modern flats

Tallest building: The Shard (310 m)

UNIT 2.4 **Numbers**

Many students are required to write clearly and accurately about statistical data. This unit explains and practises the basic language of numbers and percentages, while presenting data in charts and tables is dealt with in Unit 2.10.

1 The language of numbers

In introductions, numbers are often used to give an accurate account of a situation:

> *Approximately 1,800 children between the ages of five and 12 years were selected.*

> *The earth's atmosphere appears to be gaining 3.3 billion metric tons of carbon annually.*

Figures and **numbers** are both used to talk about statistical data in a general sense:

> *The **figures/numbers** in the report need to be read critically.*

But number is used more widely:

> *She forgot her mobile phone **number**.*

Digits are individual numbers:

> *4,539 is a four-**digit** number.*

Both **fractions** (½) and **decimals** (0.975) may be used.

There is no final 's' on hundred/thousand/million used with whole numbers:

> Six **million** people live there.

but: **Thousands** of people were forced to move from the area of the dam.

When writing about **currencies**, write *$440 m.* (440 million dollars).

Rates are normally expressed as percentages (e.g. *the literacy rate rose to 75%*) but may also be per thousand (e.g. *the Austrian birth rate is 8.7*).

It is normal to write whole numbers as words from one to ten and as digits above ten:

> There were 16 students in the class, but only eight came to the lecture.

2 Percentages

These are commonly used for expressing rates of change:

> Since 2008 the number of prisoners has risen by 22%.

■ Complete the following sentences using the data in the table below.

a) Between 2010 and 2011, the number of students increased by _____%.

b) The number increased by _____% the following year.

c) Between 2010 and 2013 there was a _____% increase.

Students studying Law and Politics 2010–2013

2010	2011	2012	2013
200	300	600	1000

3 Further numerical phrases

Too much statistical data can make a text difficult to read. In some cases, it is not necessary to give exact numbers. The expressions listed below can also be used to present and simplify statistical information. Compare:

> The course fees rose from $1,200 to $2,500 in two years.

> The course fees **doubled** in two years.

If appropriate, *roughly/approximately* can be added:

> *The course fees **roughly doubled** in two years.*

The following phrases are widely used:

one in three	***One in three** engineering students is from China.*
twice/three times as many	***Twice as many** women as men study business law.*
a five/tenfold increase	*There was a **fivefold increase** in the price of oil.*
to double/halve	*The rate of infection **halved** after 2001.*
the highest/lowest	***The lowest** rate of home ownership was in Germany.*
a quarter/fifth	*A **fifth** of all employees leave every year.*
the majority/minority	***The majority** of births are in hospital.*
on average/the average	***On average**, each judge hears two cases per day.*
a small/large proportion	*The website generates **a large proportion** of their sales.*

NB: 5–20% = a small minority   51–55% = a small majority
     21–39% = a minority   56–79% = a majority
     40–49% = a substantial/significant minority 80%+ = a large majority

■ **Rewrite each sentence in a simpler way, using a suitable expression from the list above.**

a) In 1975 a litre of petrol cost 12p, while the price is now £1.20.

b) Out of 18 students in the group 12 were women.

c) The new high-speed train reduced the journey time to Madrid from seven hours to three hours 20 minutes.

d) The number of students applying for the Psychology course has risen from 350 last year to 525 this year.

e) More than 80% of British students complete their first degree course; in Italy the figure is just 35%.

f) Tap water costs 0.07p per litre while bottled water costs, on average, 50p per litre.

g)   The rate of unemployment ranges from 24% in Spain to 3% in Norway.

h)   57% of the members supported the suggestion, but 83% of these had some doubts.

4 Practice A

■ Study the data in the table below and write sentences using suitable numerical phrases.

Selected Olympic Games 1896–2008

Year	Host	Sports	Events	Athletes	% Women
1896	Athens	9	43	241	0.0%
1924	Paris	17	126	3,089	4.4%
1964	Tokyo	19	163	5,151	13.2%
1992	Barcelona	32	257	9,356	28.9%
2008	Beijing	28	302	10,942	42.4%

a)   *At the Paris Olympics in 1924 a small minority of athletes were female.*

b)   _____

c)   _____

d)   _____

e)   _____

f)   _____

5 Practice B

■ The following data were collected about a group of 15 international students. Write a paragraph about the group using the data.

Mother tongue		Future course		Age		Favourite sport	
Arabic	2	Accounting	1	21	1	Climbing	2
Chinese	8	Economics	3	22	3	Cycling	1
French	1	Finance	2	23	9	Dancing	3
Japanese	1	Management	6	24	–	Football	3
Korean	2	MBA	2	25	–	Swimming	5
Spanish	1	Tourism	1	26	1	Tennis	1

■ Write a few sentences about the students in your class.

UNIT 2.5 Passives

The passive form is a feature of much academic writing, making it more impersonal and formal, but the passive should not be overused. This unit provides practice in developing a balanced style.

1 Active and passive

The passive is used when the writer wants to focus on the result, not on the cause. Compare:

> **Walter Trimble** *founded the college in 1925.* (active)

> **The college** *was founded in 1925 by Walter Trimble.* (passive)

In the first sentence, the emphasis is on Trimble, in the second on the college. So the passive is often used in written English when the cause (a person or thing) is less important or unknown:

> *Aluminium **was first produced** in the nineteenth century.* (by someone)

If necessary, the cause of the action can be shown by adding 'by . . .':

> *The city was flooded **by a severe hurricane**.*

The passive is also used in written work to provide a more impersonal style:

> *The findings **were evaluated**.* (not 'I evaluated the findings')

2 Structure

All passive structures have two parts:

Form of the verb 'to be'	Past participle
is	constructed
was	developed
will be	reorganised

■ Change the following from active to passive.

a)   We collected the data and compared the two groups.

b)   I interviewed 120 people in three social classes.

c)   They checked the results and found several errors.

d)   We will make an analysis of the findings.

e)   He asked four doctors to give their opinions.

f)   She wrote the report and distributed ten copies.

3 Using adverbs

An adverb can be inserted in a passive form to add information:

*The machinery was used **regularly** until 1938.*

*This process is **commonly** called 'networking'.*

■ Change the following sentences from active to passive and insert a suitable adverb from the box below. Decide if it is necessary to show a cause, and if so, add it.

Example:
  The recession forced half the companies to close down. (active)
  *Half the companies were **eventually** forced to close down by the recession.* (passive)

a)   The Connors family ran the company until 1981.

b)   Dr Weber has predicted that prisons will be unnecessary in the future.

c) They provided pencils for all students in the exam.

d) The researchers calculated the percentages to three decimal places.

e) The students handed in the essays on Tuesday morning.

---

optimistically   helpfully   punctually   accurately
eventually   profitably

---

4 Practice

In most texts, the active and the passive are mixed, to produce a balanced style.

■ **Read the following description of the early years of the Boots company and underline the passive forms.**

BOOTS

When John Boot died at the young age of 45, he was worn out by the effort of establishing his herbal medicine business in Nottingham. He had spent his early years as a farm labourer, but he had worked his way up to be the owner of a substantial business. He was born in 1815, became a member of a Methodist chapel in Nottingham, and later moved to the town. John was concerned by the situation of poor people who could not afford a doctor, and in 1849 he opened a herbal medicine shop, which was impressively called the British and American Botanic Establishment. In the early stages John was helped financially by his father in law, while his own mother provided herbal knowledge.

On his death in 1860 the business was taken over by his wife, and she was soon assisted by their 10-year-old son, Jesse. He quickly showed the business ability which transformed his father's shop into a national business. Jesse Boot opened more shops in poor districts of Nottingham and other towns, and pioneered advertising methods. He also insisted on doing business in cash, rather than offering his customers credit. His business was so successful that when he died in 1931 he had been created Baron Trent.

■ List the passives in the table below. Decide if the active could be used instead, and rewrite it if so.

Passive	Active possible?	Active
He was worn out	Yes	The effort ... had worn him out

■ What would be the effect of using the passive throughout the text?

Prepositions

Prepositions are generally short words such as 'by' or 'at', which have a variety of uses. They are important because different prepositions can change the meaning of a sentence. This unit explains how they can be understood and used, linking them to nouns, adjectives and verbs.

1 Types of prepositions

The use of prepositions may appear confusing, but it is best learnt by studying how certain prepositions are linked to nouns, verbs and adjectives, statements of place and time, and many common phrases such as 'on average'.

■ Underline the prepositions in the following text.

This essay sets <u>out</u> the main reasons for the growth of 'mega cities' in Asia in the twentieth century. The development of the transport network is relevant to this study, in particular the contribution made by railway building. The expansion of Tokyo and Calcutta will be examined in detail.

■ The table lists the main ways of using prepositions. Find one example of each in the text.

Noun + preposition	
Verb + preposition	
Adjective + preposition	
Phrasal verb	*sets out*
Preposition of place	
Preposition of time	
Phrase	

Note the difference between phrasal verbs and verbs with prepositions:

*The contribution **made by** railway building* (verb + preposition = easier to understand)

*The researcher **made up** some of his data* (phrasal verb = harder to understand)

2 Practice A

■ Study these further examples of preposition use and decide on their type.

a)   There are a number **of** limitations to be considered.   (*noun +*)

b)   The results would be applicable **to** all children.   (_____)

c)   The data were gathered **from** a questionnaire.   (_____)

d)   All the items were placed **within** their categories.   (_____)

e)   The results **of** the investigation are still pertinent.   (_____)

f)   The respondents had spent **on** average 4.9 years abroad.   (_____)

3 Prepositions and nouns

■ Insert a suitable preposition before or after the nouns in the sentences below.

a)   Evidence is presented in support _____ the value of women's work.

b) A small change _____ wind direction can lead to large temperature changes.

c) Many examples _____ tax evasion were found.

d) The answer _____ the problem was 0.585.

e) The second point is their impact _____ developing countries.

4 Prepositions in phrases

■ Complete the following phrases with the correct preposition.

a) _____ the whole

b) point _____ view

c) in respect _____

d) _____ spite of

e) in support _____

f) _____ the other hand

g) _____ order to

h) standard _____ living

5 Prepositions of place and time

Note the difference between 'among' and 'between':

Among 14 students in the class, only two were from Africa.
(large group)

He divided his time between the offices in Barcelona and Madrid.
(limited number)

■ Complete the following sentences with suitable prepositions of place or time.

a) _____ the respondents, few had any experience of working abroad.

b) The illiteracy rate declined gradually _____ 1976 _____ 1985.

c) Most workers _____ the European Union retire before the age _____ 60.

d) Leonardo da Vinci was born _____ Florence _____ 1452.

e) Chocolate sales fall _____ summer and peak _____ Christmas.

f) _____ the surface, there is no difference _____ male and female responses.

g) The countries _____ the Mediterranean held a meeting _____ May 20th.

6 Verbs and prepositions

The following verbs are generally used with these prepositions:

Verb + prep.	Example
add to	*The bad weather **added to** the team's difficulties.*
agree with	*Yu (1997) **agrees with** Martin and Jenks (1989).*
associate with	*Monetarism is an economic policy **associated with** Mrs Thatcher.*
believe in	*The survey showed that 65% **believed in** life after death.*
blame for	*He **blamed** unfair questions **for** his poor exam results.*
concentrate on (also: focus on)	*She dropped all her hobbies to **concentrate on** her work.*
consist of	*Parliament **consists of** two Houses: the Commons and the Lords.*
depend on (also: rely on)	*The company **depends on** IT for a rapid flow of sales data.*
derive from	*Modern computers **derive from** wartime decoding machines.*
divide into	*Trees are **divided into** two main types: conifers and deciduous.*
invest in	*Far more money needs to be **invested in** primary education.*
learn from	*All successful students **learn from** their mistakes.*
pay for	*Goods delivered in April must be **paid for** by June 30th.*
point out	*Goodson (2001) **points out** the dangers of generalisation.*
specialise in	*This department **specialises in** French poetry.*

7 Practice B

■ Complete the following with suitable verbs and prepositions.

a) The enquiry _____ the cause of the accident, not the consequences.

b) Dr Cracknell _____ that there were only two weeks before the deadline.

c) The theory of relativity will always be _____ Albert Einstein.

d) A football pitch is _____ two halves.

e) A series of strikes were _____ the decline in production during May.

f) Millions of men died for the cause they _____.

UNIT 2.7 Punctuation

Accurate punctuation and use of capital letters help the reader to understand exactly what the writer meant. While some aspects of punctuation, such as the use of commas, can be a matter of individual style, correct punctuation in areas such as quotation is vital.

1 Capital letters

It is difficult to give precise rules about the use of capital letters in modern English, where there is a trend to use them less. However, they should always be used in the following cases:

a) The first word in a sentence   *In the beginning . . .*
b) Days and months   *Friday 21st July*
c) Nationality words   *France and the French*
d) Names of people/places   *Dr Martin Lee from Sydney*
e) Book titles (main words only)   *Power and the State*
f) Academic subjects   *She studied Biology and Mathematics*
g) Names of organisations   *The University of East Anglia*

2 Apostrophes (')

These are mainly used in two situations:

a) to show contractions   *He's the leading authority on Hegel.*
    NB: contractions are not common in academic English

b) with possessives

The professor's secretary (singular)

Students' marks (plural words ending in 's')

Women's rights (for irregular plurals)

NB: **It's** is the contraction of **it is**

It's possible the course will be cancelled.

The possessive form is **its**

'Civilization and its Discontents' (Freud)

3 Semi-colons (;)

Semi-colons are used to show the link between two connected phrases, when a comma would be too weak and a full stop too strong:

Nobody questioned the results; they were quite conclusive.

Semi-colons are also used to divide up items in a list when they have a complex structure, as in a multiple citation:

(Maitland, 2006; Rosenor, 1997; New Scientist, 2006b; University of Michigan, 2000).

4 Colons (:)

Colons are used in three main ways:

a) to introduce explanations

The meeting was postponed: the Dean was ill.

b) to start a list

Two aspects were identified: financial and social.

c) to introduce a quotation

As the Duchess of Windsor said: 'You can never be too rich or too thin'.

5 Commas (,)

These are one of the commonest punctuation marks, but also the hardest to provide guidance for. It is useful to think of commas as providing a brief pause for readers, to give them a chance to make sense of a chunk of text. Comma use is partly a matter of individual style. Overuse can slow down the reader, but equally the lack of commas can be confusing.

Some instances of necessary comma usage are:

a)   after introductory words or phrases:

However, more cases should be considered before reaching a conclusion.

b)   around examples or comments:

Nationalism, it is widely recognised, has a positive and negative side.

c)   with conjunctions that separate two clauses in a sentence:

Three hundred people were interviewed, but only half the responses could be used.

d)   in lists:

Tomatoes, beans, cabbages and potatoes were all genetically modified in turn.

6 Quotations marks/inverted commas (" "/' ')

a)   Single quotation marks are used to emphasise a word:

The word 'factory' was first used in the seventeenth century.

to give quotations from other writers:

Goodwin's (1977) analysis of habit indicates that, in general, 'It will be more difficult to reverse a trend than to accentuate it'.

to show direct speech:

'Can anyone find the answer?' asked the lecturer.

Longer quotations are usually indented (i.e. have a wider margin) and/or are set in smaller type.

b)   Double quotation marks are used to show quotations inside quotations (nested quotations):

As Kauffman remarked: 'his concept of "internal space" requires close analysis'.

NB: American English uses double quotation marks to show standard quotations.

c)   In references, quotation marks are used for the names of articles and chapters, but book or journal titles normally use italics:

Russell, T. (1995) 'A future for coffee?' *Journal of Applied Marketing* 6, 14–17.

7 Full stops (.)

These are used to show the end of a sentence:

> *The first chapter provides a clear introduction to the topic.*

They are also used with certain abbreviations, when they are the first part of a word:

> *govt./Jan./p.397*

But do not use full stops with abbreviations such as:

> *BBC/UN/VIP*

8 Others

Hyphens (-) are used with certain words, such as compound nouns, and certain structures:

> *A well-researched, thought-provoking book.*

> *Her three-year-old daughter is learning to read.*

Exclamation marks (!) and question marks (?):

> *'Well!' he shouted, 'who would believe it?'*

Brackets or parentheses ( ) can be used to give additional detail, without interfering with the flow of the main idea:

> *Relatively few people (10–15%) were literate in sixteenth-century Russia.*

9 Practice A

■ Punctuate the following sentences.

a) the study was carried out by christine zhen-wei qiang of the national university of singapore

b) professor rowans new book the end of privacy 2014 is published in new york

c) as keynes said its better to be roughly right than precisely wrong

d) three departments law business and economics have had their funding cut

e)   thousands of new words such as app enter the english language each year

f)   the bbcs world service is broadcast in 33 languages including somali and vietnamese

g)   she scored 56% on the main course the previous semester she had achieved 67%

10 Practice B

■ Punctuate the following text.

the school of biomedical sciences at borchester university is offering two undergraduate degree courses in neuroscience this year students can study either neuroscience with pharmacology or neuroscience with biochemistry there is also a masters course which runs for four years and involves a period of study abroad during november and december professor andreas fischer is course leader for neuroscience and enquiries should be sent to him via the website

Singular or Plural?

In written English, the choice of singular or plural can be confusing in various situations, such as with noun/verb agreement or in the use of countable and uncountable nouns. This unit illustrates the main areas of difficulty and provides practice with these.

1 Five areas of difficulty

The main problem areas for international students are shown below.

a) Nouns should agree with verbs, and pronouns with nouns:

> *Those problems are unique*
>
> *There are many arguments in favour*

b) Uncountable nouns and irregular plurals usually have no final 's':

> *Most students receive free tuition*
>
> *The main export is tropical fruit*

c) General statements normally use the plural:

> *State universities have lower fees*

d) 'Each/every' are followed by singular noun and verb forms:

> *Every student gets financial support*

e) Two linked nouns should agree:

> *Both the similarities and differences are important*

■ Find the mistake in the following and decide what type (a–e above) it is.

a) The proposal has both advantages and disadvantage. (____)

b) A majority of children in Thailand is vaccinated against measles. (____)

c) There are few young people in rural area. (____)

d) Many places are experiencing an increase in crimes. (____)

e) Each companies have their own policies. (____)

2 Group phrases

■ Study the following 'group' phrases:

*Half the universities **are raising their fees.***	(plural verb)
***Three** areas of enquiry **were** explored.*	(plural verb)
*A **range** of courses **is** offered in Electrical Engineering.*	(singular verb)
***One** of the options **involves** spending a year abroad.*	(singular verb)

Note that if a verb has more than one subject, it must be plural, even if the preceding noun is singular:

*Scores of students, some teachers and the president **are** at the meeting*

*Their valuable suggestions and hard work **were** vital*

Certain 'group' nouns (e.g. team/army/government) can be followed by either a singular or plural verb:

*The team **was** defeated three times last month* (collectively)

*The team **were** travelling by train and bus* (separately)

3 Uncountable nouns

a) Most nouns in English are countable, but the following are generally uncountable (i.e. they are not usually used with numbers or the plural 's'):

accommodation	*information*	*scenery*
advice	*knowledge*	*staff*
behaviour	*money*	*traffic*

commerce	*news*	*travel*
data	*permission*	*trouble*
education	*progress*	*vocabulary*
equipment	*research*	*weather*
furniture	*rubbish*	*work*

Many of these can be 'counted' by using an extra noun:

A piece of advice

Three patterns of behaviour

An item of equipment

b)   Another group of uncountable nouns is used for materials:

wood/rubber/iron/coffee/paper/water/oil/stone

*Little **wood** is used in the construction of motor vehicles.*

*Huge amounts of **paper** are needed to produce these magazines.*

Many of these nouns can be used as countable nouns with a rather different meaning:

*Over twenty daily **papers** are published in Delhi.*

*Most **woods** are home to a wide variety of birds.*

c)   The most difficult group can be used either as countable or uncountable nouns, often with quite different meanings (further examples: business/capital/experience):

*She developed **an interest** in genetics. (countable)*

*The bank is paying 4% **interest**. (uncountable)*

Other nouns with a similar pattern are used for general concepts (e.g. love/fear/hope)

*Most people feel that **life** is too short. (uncountable – in general)*

*Nearly twenty **lives** were lost in the mining accident. (countable – in particular)*

4 Practice A

■ **Choose the correct alternative in these sentences.**

a)   <u>Little/few</u> news about the accident was released.

b)   He established three successful <u>businesses/business</u> in 2013.

c)   Substantial <u>experiences/experience</u> of report writing <u>are/is</u> required.

d)   It is often claimed that <u>travel broadens/travels broaden</u> the mind.

e)   How <u>much advice/many advices</u> were they given before coming to Australia?

f)   She had <u>little interest/few interests</u> outside her work.

g)   The insurance policy excludes the effects of civil <u>war/wars</u>.

h)   They studied the <u>work/works</u> of three groups of employees over two years.

5 Practice B

■ **Read the text and choose the correct alternative.**

A high percentage of <u>company/companies</u> <u>has/have</u> developed <u>website/websites</u> in the last few years. Trading using the internet is called <u>e-commerce/e-commerces</u>, and <u>this/these</u> <u>is/are</u> divided into two main kinds: B2B and B2C. The former involves trading between <u>business/businesses</u>, but many <u>company/companies</u> want to use the internet to sell directly to <u>its/their</u> customers (B2C). However, large numbers have experienced <u>trouble/troubles</u> with <u>security/securities</u> and other practical issues. In addition, the high start-up costs and the <u>expense/expenses</u> of advertising <u>means/mean</u> that <u>this/these</u> <u>company/companies</u> often struggle to make a profit.

UNIT 2.9 Time Markers

When describing a sequence of events, it is important to be clear about whether something has finished or is still in progress. Words such as 'during' and 'since' are often used to explain the timing of events, but their application may be restricted to particular tenses. This unit explains and practises their use.

1 How time markers are used

■ Study the following:

She went on a training course **for** six weeks.	(with numbers, without start date)
The report must be finished **by** June 12th.	(on or before)
He has been President **since** 2007.	(with present perfect, must specify start date)
They are studying in Bristol **until** March.	(end of a period)
The library was opened two years **ago**.	(usually with past)
The hotel is closed **during** the winter.	(with noun)
Before writing he studied over 100 sources.	(often followed by -ing form; also **after**)
He applied in May and was accepted two months **later**.	(often used with numbers; also **earlier**)

2 Tenses

■ Compare the tenses used with the following time markers:

Last year *there* **was** *an election*
in Spain.   (past – finished event)

In the last year *there* **has been** *a*   (present perfect – unfinished)
decline in inflation.

Recently, *there* **has been** *a sharp*
rise in internet use.   (present perfect – unfinished)

Currently, *there* **is** *widespread*   (present – focus on now)
concern about plagiarism.

3 Practice A

■ Choose the best alternative in each case.

a) Currently/recently she has been researching the life cycle of a Brazilian wasp.

b) He worked there until/during he retired.

c) Dr Hoffman has lived in Melbourne since/for sixteen years.

d) Last month/in the last month a new book was published on genetics.

e) Applications must be received by/on November 25th.

f) Since/during her arrival last May she has reorganised the department.

4 Practice B

■ Study the schedule for Professor Wang's recent trip and complete the sentences below with a suitable word. It is now April 16th.

March 12	Fly London – Barcelona
March 13–14	Conference in Barcelona
March 15	Train Barcelona – Paris
March 16	Lecture visit to Sorbonne
March 17	Fly Paris – Shanghai
March 18–19	Meeting with colleagues
March 20	Fly Shanghai – London

a)   _____ month Professor Wang made a lengthy trip.

b)   _____ her trip she visited three countries.

c)   _____ March 18th she had travelled 11,000 kilometres.

d)   She was away from home _____ nine days altogether.

e)   A month _____ she was in Paris.

f)   Two days _____ she was in Shanghai.

g)   She stayed in Shanghai _____ March 20th.

h)   _____ she is writing a report on her trip.

5 Practice C

■ Study the details of Napoleon's life, and write a short biography.

1769	Born in Corsica
1784	Entered military school in Paris
1789	French revolution started
1793	Promoted to brigadier general
1796	Appointed to command army of Italy; married Josephine
1799	Returned from Egypt and became First Consul of France
1807	France controlled most of continental Europe
1810	Divorced Josephine and married Marie-Louise, daughter of Austrian emperor
1812	Forced to retreat from Russia
1814	Exiled to island of Elba
1815	Defeated at battle of Waterloo and exiled to island of St Helena
1821	Died in exile

UNIT 2.10 Visual Information

In many subjects, it is essential to support your writing with statistical data. Visual devices such as graphs and tables are a convenient way of displaying large quantities of information in a form that is easy to understand. This unit explains and practises the language connected with these devices.

1 Types of visuals

There are examples of some of the main types of visuals used in academic texts on p. 160.

■ Complete the box below to show the main use (a–g) and the example (A–G) of each type.

Uses: a) location   b) comparison   c) proportion
          d) structure   e) changes in time   f) statistical display
          g) sequence of
             process

Types	Uses	Example
1 Diagram		
2 Table		
3 Map		
4 Pie chart		
5 Flow chart		
6 Line graph		
7 Bar chart		

A. Cinema ticket sales

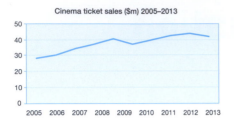

Cinema ticket sales ($m) 2005–2013

B. Average life expectancy (in years)

Japan	81.6
France	79.0
United States	77.1
South Korea	75.5
Ghana	57.9
South Africa	47.7
Kenya	44.6
Zimbabwe	33.1

C. Electricity output from coal

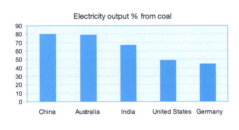

Electricity output % from coal

D. Origins of international students

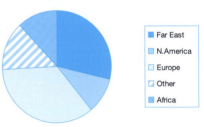

- Far East
- N.America
- Europe
- Other
- Africa

E. Planning an essay

Study wording of title → Brainstorm ideas → Read sources → Write draft outline

F. Organisation of the research unit

Director
Manager
Deputy Director
Technical Staff
Secretarial Staff
Research Staff

G. Position of the main library

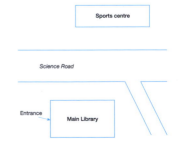

Sports centre
Science Road
Entrance
Main Library

2 The language of change

(past tenses in brackets)

Verb ⟋	Adverb	Verb ⟍	Adjective + noun
grow (grew)	*slightly*	*drop (dropped)*	*a slight drop*
rise (rose)	*gradually*	*fall (fell)*	*a gradual fall*
increase (increased)	*steadily*	*decrease (decreased)*	*a sharp decrease*
climb (climbed)	*sharply*	*decline (declined)*	*a steady decline*
also: a peak, to peak, a plateau, to level off, a trough			

*Average temperatures **rose steadily** until 2012 and then **dropped slightly**.*

*There was a **sharp decrease** in sales during the summer and then **a gradual rise**.*

■ Study the graph below and complete the description with phrases from the table above.

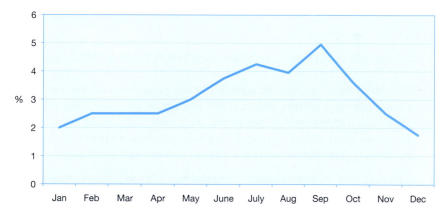

Figure 1 Inflation January–December

The graph shows that the rate of inflation was 2% in January, and then a) _____ to 2.5% in February. After that it b) _____ until April, and then c) _____ d) _____ to over 4% in July. Inflation fell e) _____ in August, but f) _____ to a g) _____ of 5% in September. Subsequently, it h) _____ i) _____ to below 2% in December.

3 Describing visuals

Although visuals do largely speak for themselves, it is common to help the reader interpret them by briefly commenting on their main features.

The graph map diagram	shows illustrates displays	the changes in the price of oil since 1990. the main sources of copper in Africa. the organisation of both companies.

■ Read the following descriptions of the chart below. Which is better, and why?

i)   The chart (Fig. 2) shows the quantity of tea consumed by the world's leading tea consuming nations. India and China together consume more than half the world's tea production, with India alone consuming about one third. Other significant tea consumers are Turkey, Russia and Britain. 'Others' includes the United States, Iran and Egypt.

ii)   The chart (Fig. 2) shows that 31% of the world's tea is consumed by India, 23% by China, and 8% by Turkey. The fourth largest consumers are Russia, Japan and Britain, with 7% each, while Pakistan consumes 5%. Other countries account for the remaining 12%.

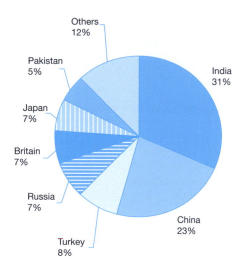

Fig. 2 World tea consumption

(Source: The Tea Council)

4 Labelling

- When referring to visual information in the text, the word 'figure' is used for almost everything (such as maps, charts and graphs) except tables (see examples above).
- Figures and tables should be numbered and given a title. Titles of tables are written above, while titles of figures are written below the data.
- As with other data, sources must be given for all visual information.
- If you are writing a lengthy work such as a dissertation, you will need to provide lists of tables and figures, showing numbers, titles and page numbers, after the contents page.

5 Practice A

■ Complete the following description of the table below (one word per gap).

Table 1 Projected population changes in various European countries 2015–2050 (millions)

Country	Population 2015	Population 2050	Change
France	62	67	+ 5
Germany	82	71	– 11
Italy	60	57	– 3
Poland	38	32	– 6
Portugal	10.7	10	– 0.7
Russia	140	116	– 24
Spain	45	51	+ 6
UK	61	72	+ 11

(Source: UN)

The table a) _____ the projected population changes in

b) _____ European countries c) _____

2015 and 2050. It can be seen that in a d) _____ the

population is expected to fall, in some cases (e.g. Germany and

Russia) quite e) _____. However, the population of

France, f) _____ and the UK is predicted to increase, in

the case of the last two by more g) _____ 10%.

6 Practice B

■ Write a paragraph commenting on the data in the table below.

Table 2 Student survey of library facilities: % students rating facilities as good

Library facilities	Undergraduates (%)	Postgraduates (%)
Opening hours	72	63
Staff helpfulness	94	81
Ease of using electronic catalogue	65	87
Availability of working space	80	76
Café area	91	95
Availability of short loan stock	43	35
Quality of main book stock	69	54

(Source: Author)

Writing Models

Reports

Although essays are the most common assignments in many academic disciplines, students of science and business are often asked to write reports. Reports and essays are similar in many ways, but this section explains and illustrates the differences.

1 Writing reports

While essays are often concerned with abstract or theoretical subjects, a report is a description of a situation or something that has happened. In academic terms, it might describe:

a) an experiment you have conducted

b) a survey you have carried out

c) a comparison of alternative proposals to deal with a situation

Clearly, there is a big difference between describing a scientific laboratory experiment and reporting on students' political opinions. In some areas (e.g. laboratory work), your teachers will make it clear what format you should follow. However, most reports should include the following features:

Introduction

- background to the subject
- reasons for carrying out the work
- review of other research in the area

Methods

- how you did your research
- description of the tools/materials used

Results

- what you discovered
- comments on likely accuracy of results

Discussion

- of your main findings
- comments on the effectiveness of your research

Conclusion

- summary of your work
- suggestions for further research

2 Essays and reports

In comparison with essays, reports are likely to:

a) be based on primary as well as secondary research
b) use numbering (1.2, 1.2) and subheadings for different sections
c) be more specific and detailed

In most other respects, reports are similar to essays, since both:

a) have a clear and logical format
b) use objective and accurate academic style
c) include citations and references
d) make use of visual information in the form of graphs and tables
e) include appendices where necessary

■ Decide whether the following topics are more likely to be written as reports or essays.

Topic	Report	Essay
1 The development of trade unions in South Africa		
2 Two alternative plans for improving the sports centre		
3 A study you conducted to compare male and female attitudes to eating		
4 An overview of recent research on the human genome		
5 The arguments for and against capital punishment		

3 Survey report

■ Study the report of a survey carried out on a university campus. Complete the report by inserting suitable words from the box below into the gaps (more words than gaps).

> sample   conducted   method   respondents   random   questions
> majority   questioned   mentioned   interviewees   common
> questionnaire   unusual   generally   minority   slightly

Student experience of part-time work

Introduction

   With the introduction of course fees and the related increase in student debt, more students are finding it necessary to work part-time. The survey was a) _____ to find out how this work affects student life and study.

Method

   The research was done by asking students selected at b) _____ on the campus to complete a c) _____ (see Appendix 1). 50 students were d) _____ on Saturday April 23rd, with approximately equal numbers of male and female students.

Table 1 Do you have, or have you had, a part-time job?

	Men	Women	Total	%
Have job now	8	7	15	30
Had job before	4	6	10	20
Never had job	14	11	25	50

Findings

Of the e) _____, 30% currently had part-time jobs, 20% had had part-time jobs, but half had never done any work during university semesters (see Table 1). f) _____ who were working or who had worked were next asked about their reasons for taking the jobs. The most common reason was lack of money (56%), but many students said that they found the work useful experience (32%) and others g) _____ social benefits (12%).

The 25 students with work experience were next asked about the effects of the work on their studies. A significant h) _____ (64%) claimed that there were no negative effects at all. However, 24% said that their academic work suffered i) _____, while a small j) _____ (12%) reported serious adverse results, such as tiredness in lectures and falling marks.

Further k) _____ examined the nature of the work that the students did. The variety of jobs was surprising, from van driver to busker, but the most l) _____ areas were catering and bar work (44%) and secretarial work (32%). Most students worked between 10 and 15 hours per week, though two (8%) worked over 25 hours. Rates of pay were m) _____ near the national minimum wage, and averaged £6.20 per hour.

The final question invited students to comment on their experience of part-time work. Many (44%) made the point that students should be given larger grants so that they could concentrate on their studies full-time, but others felt that they gained something from the experience, such as meeting new people and getting insights into various work environments. One student said that she had met her current boyfriend while working in a city centre restaurant.

Conclusions

It is clear that part-time work is now a common aspect of student life. Many students find jobs at some point in their studies, but an overwhelming majority (88%) of those deny that it has a damaging effect on their studies. Most students work for only 2–3 hours per day on average, and a significant number claim some positive results from their employment. Obviously, our survey was limited to a relatively small n) _____ by time constraints, and a fuller study might modify our findings in various ways.

4 Practice

The plans below illustrate two proposals for redeveloping a site on a university campus.

■ **Study the plans and then read the five sentences (a–e), which are the introduction to a report on the redevelopment. The order of the sentences has been mixed up. Put them in the correct order. Then write the rest of the report in about 250 words.**

Plan A

Access road

| Tennis courts | Park area
Trees and seats | Car park
20 spaces |

Plan B

Access road

Car park
50 spaces

Café and shops

Swimming pool
with changing rooms

a)   The report takes into account a consultation exercise with staff and students carried out last autumn.

b)   Two alternatives schemes for redevelopment have been put forward, as can be seen in Plans A and B above.

c)   This report attempts to compare the two schemes on this basis and to establish which is the more suitable.

d)   The aim of the redevelopment is to improve facilities for both staff and students, and at the same time enhance the appearance of this part of the campus.

e)   Due to the recent closure of the maintenance depot, a site approximately 250 metres long and 100 metres wide has recently become vacant on the west side of the university campus.

5 Scientific reports

Scientific research

This is usually conducted in order to support a hypothesis or to validate the work of others. An accurate written record of the experiment is important because it allows other researchers to share your work. At graduate level or above, your research is adding to an international body of data on your particular area of study.

In general, scientific reports follow the same guidelines as other academic writing in terms of style and vocabulary. However, your department may well have its own requirements, for example the organisation of a report, so it is advisable to ask if these exist.

Format

Reports of laboratory experiments in disciplines such as biology, chemistry and physics generally include the following sections:

a)   Title

This should contain the essential elements of the report in (ideally) no more than 12 words:

The effect of temperature changes on the germination of wheat (*Triticum aestivum*)

b) Abstract

The function of an abstract is to help a potential reader identify whether your report is relevant to his/her research interests. It is essentially a summary in about 200 words of each part of the report, and so it is commonly written after the last draft is finalised. It should include the principal conclusions, and be written in the same tenses as the main report.

c) Introduction

The introduction should contextualise your work with reference to other similar research. It should cite previous research papers that you have studied, in order to explain the purpose of your work (e.g. to confirm or extend their findings). It must contain a purpose statement (why you did this experiment) or a hypothesis you wished to evaluate, or both.

d) Method

This section explains how you did the research. It should allow another researcher to repeat your work, so it needs to include a description of equipment and materials used, as well as the process you followed. You may wish to include diagrams or photographs to illustrate the set-up in the laboratory. The passive is normally used (three samples were prepared) rather than the active (we prepared . . .). As the research is concluded, the past tense should be used throughout.

e) Results

Again using the past tense, here you summarise all the results obtained. Detailed data may be presented in tables and graphs, with only the most important features highlighted in the text. You must include all results, including unexpected ones that do not conform to your hypothesis.

f) Discussion

This section links back to the introduction by comparing your results with the original purpose or hypothesis. It aims to evaluate the experiment in terms of your findings and compare them to your expectations. It may be necessary to refer to the relevant literature. The conclusion should make it clear whether you feel that your hypothesis has been supported, and if there are changes that you would make to the design of the experiment if you were to repeat it.

g) References

As in all academic writing, this is a list of all the sources you have specifically mentioned in your report.

UNIT 3.2 Longer Essays

Long essays of 2,500–5,000 words may be required as part of a module assessment. These require more research and organisation than short essays, and this section provides a guide to how such an assignment can be tackled.

1 Planning your work

Longer assignments are normally set many weeks before their deadline, which means that students should have plenty of time to organise their writing. However, it is worth remembering that at the end of a semester you may have to complete several writing tasks, so it may be a good idea to finish one earlier.

You should also check the submission requirements of your department. These include style of referencing, method of submission (i.e. electronic, hard copy or both) and place and time of submission. Being clear about these will avoid last-minute panic.

a) The first thing is to prepare a schedule for your work. An eight-week schedule might look like this:

Week	Stages of work	Relevant units in this book
1	Study title and make first outline. Look for and evaluate suitable sources.	1.5
2	Reading and note-making. Keep record of all sources used.	1.2, 1.3, 1.6, 1.8
3	Reading, note-making, paraphrasing and summarising. Modify outline.	1.2, 1.3, 1.6, 1.7

4	Write draft of main body.	1.9, 1.10
5	Write draft introduction and conclusion.	1.11
6	Rewrite introduction, main body and conclusion, checking for logical development of ideas and relevance to title.	1.12
7	Organise list of references, contents, list of figures and appendices if required. Check all in-text citations.	1.8
8	Proofread the whole essay before handing it in. Make sure that the overall presentation is clear and accurate.	1.12

b) How you actually plan your schedule is up to you, but the important thing is to organise your time effectively. Leaving the writing stage until the last minute will not lead to a good mark, however much research you have done. Although you may be tempted to postpone writing, the sooner you start, the sooner you will be able to begin refining your ideas. Remember that late submission of coursework is usually penalised.

c) Longer papers may include the following features, in this order:

Title page	Apart from the title, this usually shows the student's name and module title and number.
Contents page	This should show the reader the basic organisation of the essay, with page numbers.
List of tables or figures	If the essay includes visual features such as graphs, these need to be listed by title and page number.
Introduction	
Main body	If a numbering system is used, the chief sections of the main body are normally numbered 1, 2, 3 and then subdivided 1.1, 1.2, etc.
Conclusion	
List of references	This is a complete list of all the sources cited in the text. Writers occasionally also include a bibliography, which is a list of sources read but not cited.
Appendices (singular – appendix)	These sections are for data related to the topic that the reader may want to refer to. Each appendix should have a title and be mentioned in the main body.

2 Example essay

■   Read the following essay on the topic of nuclear energy. In pairs or groups, discuss the following points:

a)   What is the writer's position on this issue?

b)   How does the writer make his/her position clear?

EVALUATE THE RISKS OF USING NUCLEAR ENERGY AS AN ALTERNATIVE TO FOSSIL FUELS

Introduction

The search for sources of energy began when humans first started to burn wood or other forms of biomass to generate heat for cooking and smelting. This was followed by using hydropower from rivers and harnessing wind energy with windmills. Later the exploitation of chemical energy began with the burning of coal, oil and natural gas. Then, in the middle of the twentieth century, nuclear energy appeared for the first time, with the hope that it would allow the efficient production of cheap, clean energy (Bodansky, 2004).

Nuclear energy has, however, become the subject of considerable debate, with its proponents claiming that it is beneficial for the environment, since its production does not create carbon dioxide (CO_2) which can lead to global warming. However, its opponents argue that it can damage the environment by creating radioactive waste. It is also linked to diseases in humans, and there is the additional fear that it may be abused by terrorists in future. These critics further argue that other energy sources, such as solar power, could constitute safer alternatives to fossil fuels without posing an environmental threat.

This essay attempts to assess the risks of using nuclear power, in comparison with other sources of energy. The main arguments for employing nuclear energy are first considered, followed by an examination of the safety issues around this source of power, including the safety and security concerns connected with nuclear waste.

1. Reasons for using nuclear energy

1.1 An alternative source of energy

The rationale behind using nuclear energy stems from the need to find alternative energy sources to fossil fuels i.e. oil, gas and coal, which are finite. This is a growing concern, due to the increase in the global population, which is accompanied by an increase in energy demand. Mathew (2006) indicates that the annual energy consumption rate per capita in developed countries is between 4,000 and 9,000 kgs of oil, while the rate in less developed countries is around 500 kgs. As a result, the demand for total primary energy, which will accompany the population growth, is projected to increase from 12.1 Mtoe (million tons of oil equivalent) to 16.1 Mtoe in 2030. If this increase occurs the total global stock of oil and gas would only be adequate for 250 years, thus requiring the urgent development of other energy sources, which would not deplete the stock of natural resources available for future generations.

1.2 Limitations of other energy sources

Wind energy and solar power are frequently presented as alternative energy sources to fossil fuels. Both are freely available in many parts of the world and their use involves no CO_2 emissions. Sterrett (1994) claims that sufficient wind energy exists to displace approximately eight billion barrels of oil. However, wind energy is unreliable, as wind turbines do not function if the wind speed is too high or low. Similarly, solar power is only effective during the day, and is uneconomic in cool and cloudy climates. Neither of these sources currently offers an efficient and reliable alternative to energy created from fossil fuels.

1.3 Reducing carbon dioxide emissions

An important reason for using nuclear energy is to reduce the emissions of CO_2, which are produced by burning fossil fuels. Bodansky (2004) points out that this type of fuel is the main source of the increase in atmospheric carbon dioxide. The amount of CO_2 produced by each source differs due to the differences in their hydrogen content. For example, natural gas contains one carbon atom and four hydrogen atoms which combine with oxygen to produce CO_2. The proportion of

CO_2 is lower than with the other sources, because the emission depends on the mass of carbon inside the chemical compounds. Although natural gas is thus cleaner than the alternatives, burning all three fuels contributes to the greenhouse effect which is causing the earth to heat up.

Nuclear energy, however, emits no carbon dioxide, sulphur dioxide (SO_2) or nitrous oxide (NOx). It is estimated that in 2003, in the USA, nuclear energy prevented the release of 680 million tons of CO_2, 3.4 millions tons of SO_2 and 1.3 million tons of NOx. If released from coal burning plants, these gases would have caused the deaths of 40,000 people annually (Olah *et al.*, 2006:127). According to Richard (2008:273) the use of nuclear energy in France between 1980 and 1987 reduced CO_2 emissions by 34%.

1.4 Cost efficiency

Nuclear energy could potentially generate more electricity than other current sources. As Murray (2000:73) explains, a typical reactor, which consumes 4 kg/day of uranium U235, generates 3,000 MW of energy a day, while other sources such as natural gas, coal or oil require many times the equivalent of that amount of uranium to generate the same energy. Therefore nuclear energy is relatively cost efficient as it uses a cheap raw material.

In recent years the price of oil and natural gas has risen sharply, and this trend seems likely to continue in future. Lillington (2004) suggests that the cost of purchasing fuel for nuclear energy is likely to remain low compared to other energy sources, so it seems likely that this cost advantage will become a significant factor in the comparison between nuclear and other energy sources.

2. Health and safety concerns

2.1 The impact of radiation on the human body

Especially since the Chernobyl accident in 1986 there has been persistent concern about the dangers to human health from nuclear power and nuclear waste. However, it must be understood that nuclear energy is not the only source of radiation, and that there are natural sources in the environment which may be more significant. According to Bodansky (2004:74) there is far more exposure to radiation from natural sources such as radon and cosmic rays than from all human sources, for example X-rays and nuclear medicine.

Some researchers argue that radon is one of the main causes of cancer diseases among uranium miners. However, radon may be found in all types of soil which contain uranium and radium. Bodansky (2004) points out that the concentration of radon in the soil depends on the type of soil. Hence people's exposure to radon depends on their surroundings, so that people living in houses made from limestone or wood are exposed to less radon than those living in houses built with granite. So it seems that it is not only uranium miners who are exposed to radiation, but also people in certain geological districts.

According to US law the maximum permissible exposure for those living close to nuclear plants is 1/200 rem. However, according to Hoyle (1979) this amount is just 1/20th of the radiation that can be experienced from natural background radiation. It has been estimated that nuclear energy is responsible for just 20 deaths per year worldwide, although these figures are disputed by anti-nuclear campaigners who claim that the true figure is as high as 600 deaths. Hoyle (ibid.) claims that the average American's life-span is reduced by 1.2 hours as a result of nuclear accidents, and contrasts that with the risk from smoking, which is a loss of eight years if one packet a day is smoked. Consequently, it can be seen that the risk to human health from the use of nuclear power is extremely low.

With regard to medical treatment, which is the next largest source of exposure to radiation, X-rays will expose a patient to radiation amounts from 0.4 to 1 rad (radiation absorbed dose). A broken wrist, for instance, is likely to require 4 X-rays with a total exposure of up to 4 rads. The unit of measurement for radiation exposure is the rem, and one rem is equal to the damage caused by one rad of X-rays; the maximum amount allowed for workers in nuclear plants is five rem per year: the same as the quantity received in the course of a routine medical check-up.

2.2 The impact of radioactive waste on the environment

Nuclear energy is not alone in producing dangerous waste. Lillington (2004) estimates that nuclear energy, in the course of producing 1000 megawatts (MWe) of electricity produces annually about 30 tons of highly radioactive waste and about 800 tons of intermediate and low-level waste. In contrast, a coal-burning plant producing the same quantity of electricity would generate about 320,000 tons of coal ash, of which nearly 400 tons would be hazardous waste such as mercury and vanadium, and at least 44,000 tons of sulphur dioxide. So it can be seen that nuclear energy only produces a fraction of the dangerous wastes emitted from coal-fired power stations, and in addition does not produce greenhouse gases.

2.3 Risks of terrorism

There has been widespread concern that terrorists might steal plutonium to produce nuclear weapons. In general nuclear facilities are tightly controlled, and in practice, it would be very difficult for terrorists to use such stolen material effectively. There are alternative materials such as toxic gas which could produce equally lethal terrorist weapons. However, these concerns could be solved by keeping U233 mixed with U238, which would prevent terrorist groups extracting the plutonium and fabricating a bomb.

Conclusion

The risks of nuclear energy in terms of both human health and the environment have been the subject of widespread debate and controversy. This essay has attempted to examine these risks both in terms of human health and environmental damage. It appears that many of these concerns are exaggerated, and that nuclear energy can be seen as a safe, reliable and cost effective alternative to using fossil fuels.

While all energy sources have drawbacks, nuclear should be viewed as a useful and relatively safe component in a mix of sources which can include renewables such as hydro and wind energy and non-renewables such as natural gas. The steady depletion of reserves of oil and the subsequent rise in prices is liable to emphasise this position.

Clearly more could be done to make nuclear plants safer and more efficient in future, but until their value is recognised and more work is done on their design and construction their full potential is unlikely to be realised.

References

Bodansky, D. (2004) *Nuclear Energy: Principles, Practices and Prospects.* New York: Springer.

Hoyle, F. (1979) *Energy or Extinction?* London: Heinemann.

Lillington, J. N. (2004) *The Future of Nuclear Power.* Oxford: Elsevier.

Mathew, S. (2006) *Wind Energy: Fundamentals, Resource Analysis and Economics.* Berlin: Springer.

Murray, L. R. (2009) *Nuclear Energy. An Introduction to the Concepts, System and Application of the Nuclear Process.* Oxford: Butterworth.

Olah, A. G., Goeppert, A., Parakash, S. (2006) *Beyond Oil and Gas: The Methanol Economy.* Wienheim: Wiley.

Sterrett, T. (1994) *The Energy Dilemma.* London: Multivox.

3 Revision

■ **Look back at the text and find examples of the following features:**

a)   Background information

b)   A purpose statement

c)   An outline

d)   A definition

e)   A generalisation

f)   The use of brackets to give extra detail

g)   A passive structure

h)   A phrase showing cause and effect

i)   A synonym for 'energy'

j)   An example of tentative or cautious language

k)   An example to support the writer's argument

l)   A counterargument

m) A citation

n)   A synopsis

NB: Formatting of written assignments

Some departments may expect essays to be written in the style illustrated above, with numbered section and headings, while other may require essays to be written without these. It is important to check with your teachers what the preferred style is.

Test Your Progress

Describing a process: writing an essay

This exercise is designed to allow students to assess their progress in academic writing.

■ **Study the flow chart below, which explains the process of writing an essay. Then complete the description of the process by adding one suitable word to each gap in the text on p. 186.**

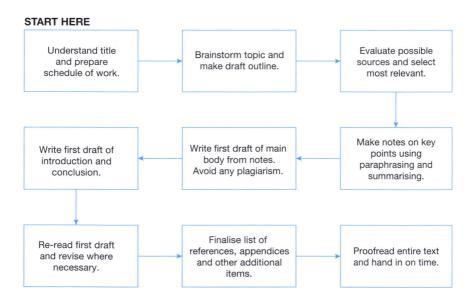

START HERE

| Understand title and prepare schedule of work. | → | Brainstorm topic and make draft outline. | → | Evaluate possible sources and select most relevant. |

| Write first draft of introduction and conclusion. | ← | Write first draft of main body from notes. Avoid any plagiarism. | ← | Make notes on key points using paraphrasing and summarising. |

| Re-read first draft and revise where necessary. | → | Finalise list of references, appendices and other additional items. | → | Proofread entire text and hand in on time. |

The first a) _____ of essay writing is to read and understand

b) _____ title, and then to prepare a schedule of work

c) _____ the available time. d) _____ the topic

should be brainstormed e) _____ a draft outline prepared.

Next, possible sources have to be evaluated f) _____ and the

most relevant selected, after g) _____ you can start making

notes, using paraphrasing and summarising h) _____. When

you have collected enough material to i) _____ the question

the first draft of the main body can j) _____ written from the

notes, k) _____ care to avoid any plagiarism. Subsequently

l) _____ can write the first draft of the introduction and

conclusion, m) _____ that a logical approach to the title is

developed. n) _____ this the whole draft must be critically

re-read and revised for o) _____ clarity and accuracy. The

penultimate stage is p) _____ prepare a final list of

references, appendices and other items such as q) _____.

Finally the whole text r) _____ be thoroughly proofread

before handing in the assignment on time.

Answers

Providing answers for a writing course is less clear-cut than for other language areas. In some exercises, there is only one possible answer, but in other cases several possibilities exist. Teachers need to use common sense, and accept any reasonable answer. In the case of exercises where students can choose their own topic and it is therefore impossible to provide a definite answer, students still appreciate having an example answer, and so some have been included.

How Much Do You Know about Academic Writing?

1   An essay is a general term for a piece of writing on a title given by the teacher. A report is usually a description of something that has happened (e.g. an experiment in the laboratory or a survey the student has conducted) (*see Unit 3.1*).

2   Conjunctions (*see Unit 1.10*).

3   Apostrophe (*see Unit 2.7*).

4   Main uses: beginning of a sentence/name of organisation/day/month/ nationality/names of people and places/titles of books. (*see Unit 2.7*).

5   Bias occurs where the writer only presents arguments for one side of a case and ignores the opposite point of view (*see Unit 1.3*).

6   True (*see Unit 1.10*).

7   Quotations can be used when they are well-known phrases, or concisely explained, or distinctively expressed (*see Unit 1.8*).

8   Child, woman, girl. The others are too informal (*see Unit 1.12*).

9   Quotations/titles (*see Unit 2.7*).

10   Proofreading means checking your work for minor errors. Rewriting is a more radical attempt to reorganise the work (*see Unit 1.12*).

11   Prefixes (*see Unit 1.2*).

12   See Unit 6 for examples.

13 At the beginning. It is a summary of an article to help a potential reader decide if it is relevant to their interests (*see Unit 1.3*).

14 To allow the reader to find the original source/to show that you have studied the relevant authorities (*see Unit 1.8*).

15 Nation/state (*see Unit 1.7*).

16 Paraphrasing mean rewriting with substantially different language. Summarising is reducing the length while retaining the main points (*see Unit 1.7*).

17 Main body (*see Unit 1.1*).

18 Uncountable nouns (*see Unit 2.1*).

19 A flow chart illustrates a process. A pie chart shows proportion (*see Unit 2.10*).

20 To give subsidiary information/to indicate citations (*see Unit 2.7*).

Part 1: Process and Skills

Unit 1.1: Introduction to Writing

1. Why do we write?

Other reasons might include:
- To present a hypothesis for consideration by others
- To make notes on something read or heard

Possibilities include:
- Semi-formal vocabulary, lack of idioms
- Use of citation/references
- Use of both passive and active

2. Types of academic writing

Notes – A written record of the main points of a text or lecture, for a student's personal use.

Report – A description of something a student has done (e.g. conducting a survey or experiment).

Project – A piece of research, either individual or group work, with the topic chosen by the student(s).

Essay – The most common type of written work, with the title given by the teacher, normally 1,000–5,000 words.

Dissertation/Thesis – The longest piece of writing normally done by a student (20,000+ words) often for a higher degree, on a topic chosen by the student.

Paper – A general term for any academic essay, report, presentation or article.

3. **The format of long and short writing tasks**

   a) abstract
   b) references
   c) appendix
   d) acknowledgements
   e) literature review
   f) case study

4. **The components of academic writing**

   (Other answers possible for a and f)

   a) There has been considerable discussion recently about the benefits of omega-3 fatty acids in the diet
   b) Introduction
   c) Misleading health claims regarding omega-3 fatty acids
   d) There has been . . . increase sales. OR: However, consumers may . . . (DHA)
   e) A fishy story
   f) It is claimed that

6. **Writing in paragraphs**

   - The purpose of a paragraph is to deal with one topic in a convenient form.
   - Texts are divided into paragraphs to help readers understand the ideas being explained by breaking the text up into suitable sections.
   - Paragraphs are normally about five or six sentences long, depending on the subject.

   para 2 begins: Despite these differences . . .
   para 3 begins: Diversification must also . . .
   para 4 begins: A further consideration is . . .

7. **Progress check**

acknowledgement	recognition of assistance given to a writer
appendix	additional information added to the end of a paper
assignment	any task given to students by their teacher
citation	a link, included in the text, to a reference
component	a part of a complete thing
dissertation	a lengthy piece of work written for a higher degree
format	the organisation or layout of a text
italics	lettering angled to the right
phrase	a group of words commonly used together
project	a piece of work on a topic chosen by the student

Unit 1.2: Reading: Assessing Sources/Using Prefixes and Suffixes

1. Types of text

(Possible answers)

Text type	Advantages	Disadvantages
Website	Usually up to date	Possibly unreliable and/or unedited
Journal article	Often focuses on a special area	May be too specialised or complex
Official report (e.g. from government)	Contains a lot of detail	May have a narrow focus
Newspaper or magazine article	Easy to read and up to date	May not be objective or give sources
E-book	Easily accessible	Must be read on screen

2. Finding suitable texts

Extract 2.1 – Yes – it summarises some relevant research, and includes citations

Extract 2.2 – No – apparently an informal personal report

Extract 2.3 – Possibly – appears to be a newspaper article but includes relevant information

4. Using library catalogues

Title 1 is up to date and appears to be a general introduction. Title 4 is a little older but seems relevant. Title 6 might also be worth examining.

6. Prefixes

auto	by itself
co	together
ex	(i) previous
	(ii) outside
fore	in front
inter	between
macro	large
micro	small
multi	many
over	too much

poly	many
post	later/after
re	again
sub	below
trans	across
under	(i) below
	(ii) not enough

7. Practice A

a)   make a guess that is too low
b)   more tickets sold than seats available
c)   very local climate
d)   economy based on information, not production
e)   disappointed

9. Practice B

a)   joint production/junior company
b)   without choosing to/not hurt
c)   able to be refilled/clear and obvious
d)   cannot be provided/unusual
e)   failure in communication/new order

10. Progress check

The text is relevant to your topic and seems to be fairly up to date. The style is quite formal but no citations are given, and there is no author given. It could be included in an essay.

inexpensive (adjective) – cheap
unmanned (adj) – without pilot
ultralight (adj) – very light
wingspan (noun) – distance from end of one wing to end of other wing
rechargeable (adj) – able to be refilled (see 9c)
undercarriage (n) – wheels used for moving on the ground
inessential (adj) – not important
subequatorial (adj) – on either side of the equator
infrastructure (n) – basic built facilities (e.g. railways, roads, power grid)

Unit 1.3: Reading: Critical Approaches/Argument and Discussion

1. Reading methods

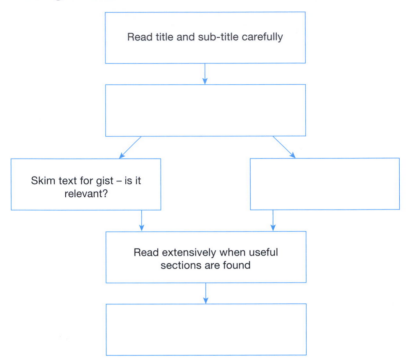

3. Reading abstracts

a) Background – A growing chorus of scholars . . . American democracy.
b) Aim and thesis of paper – This article questions . . . engaged citizenship.
c) Method of research – Using data from . . . political participation.
d) Results of research – Rather than the erosion . . . in America.

5. Critical thinking

The responses to these questions will vary from student to student, which is the nature of the critical approach.

6. Discussion vocabulary

a) benefits/advantages
b) drawbacks/disadvantages
c) negative

d)   advantages/benefits
e)   disadvantages/drawbacks
f)   benefit/advantage

8. Organisation

Vertical: a simpler pattern suitable for short essays
Horizontal: allows a more complex approach in longer essays

9. Practice

(Possible ideas)

+	–
No time wasted commuting to work	Employees may feel isolated
Gives employees more flexibility	May not suit all employees
Saves expensive office space	Home may contain distractions
Made possible by new technology	Requires different management style

(Model outline)

Drawbacks

Homeworking does not suit all employees – some may feel isolated or lack self-
    discipline

Requires different management style

Need for space and proper equipment in the home

Benefits

Employees save time and money by not commuting

Employees gain flexibility about when they work – beneficial for childcare

Employers save on office space and may gain productivity

Discussion

New technology has freed some workers from need to work in central offices

But for this to succeed employers must adopt a new approach to their workforce
    and ensure they are properly equipped

10. Counterarguments

The writer's position is essentially supportive of working from home.

(Example answers)

Counterargument	**Your position**
It has been claimed that employees may waste time at home,	but in practice there seems little evidence for this.
Although homeworking may save companies money by reducing the need for office space,	employees need to have a well-equipped workspace in their home.

11. Progress check

(Example answer)

There has been considerable debate about the value of space exploration, in view of the high costs involved. Supporters such as Donnet-Kammel (2005) claim that this is a vital method of collecting data about the structure of the universe, and additionally point out that there have been many practical benefits arising from the space programme, such as satellite communication. The example of the space station is also given as an instance of the value of the research programme in encouraging international cooperation.

In contrast, critics (e.g. Soroka, 2000) point to the huge costs involved in launching space probes, claiming that these resources would be better devoted to solving the serious earthly problems of hunger and disease. Furthermore, they argue that much of the space programme is effectively a testing ground for new weapons, such as missiles, and brings little benefit to ordinary people. In the context of the current economic crisis, a more critical approach is clearly needed in deciding which space projects have real value.

1.4 Avoiding Plagiarism/Giving Examples

3. Degrees of plagiarism

1   Y
2   Y
3   N
4   Y
5   N
6   N
7   Y

4. Avoiding plagiarism by summarising and paraphrasing

a)   Acceptable – a correctly referenced summary
b)   Plagiarised – original wording with minor changes to word order
c)   Acceptable – a correctly referenced quotation
d)   Technically plagiarism – mistake in date means the citation is incorrect

5. Avoiding plagiarism by developing good study habits

(Possible further suggestions)

- Check that quotations are exactly the same wording as the original.
- When paraphrasing, alter the structure as well as the vocabulary.
- Make sure all in-text citations are included in the list of references.

7. Phrases to introduce examples

(Example answers)

a) Some twentieth-century inventions, such as TV and the internet, affected the lives of most people.

b) Lately, many countries, for instance China, have introduced fees for university courses.

c) Various companies have built their reputation on the strength of one product: a case in point is Microsoft Windows.

d) In recent years, more women (e.g. Angela Merkel) have become political leaders.

e) Certain countries such as Japan are frequently affected by earthquakes.

f) Many musical instruments, for example guitars, use strings to make music.

8. Practice

Widespread use of the internet has led to a major change in shopping habits. It is no longer necessary to visit shops to make routine purchases, **for example many supermarkets offer delivery services for online customers**. With more specialised items **such as books and music** internet retailers can offer a wider range of products than bricks-and-mortar shops. They can also provide extra incentives to customers, **for instance free delivery or discounted prices**, in addition to the convenience of not having to visit a real shop. As a result certain types of store **(e.g. bookshops)** are disappearing from the high street. Other products, however, **for instance clothing and footwear**, appear to require personal inspection and approval, and in addition many people enjoy the activity of shopping, so it seems unlikely that the internet will completely replace the shopping centre.

9. Restatement

a) The company's overheads, in other words the fixed costs, doubled last year.

b) The Roman Empire (27 BC–AD 476) was a period of autocratic rule.

c) The Indian capital, namely New Delhi, has a thriving commercial centre.

d) Survival rates for the most common type of cancer (i.e. breast cancer) are improving.

e) Participation rates in most democracies are in decline, that is to say fewer people are voting.

10. Progress check

(Possible examples)

Customs: holidays and festivals, ways of greeting people
Everyday patterns of life: types of shop, shop opening times
Inevitable differences: language, currency
Rapid changes of mood: depression, elation
Relatively short period: two/three months
Some aspects of their new surroundings: freedom, independence, weather

Unit 1.5: Understanding Titles and Essay Planning/Showing Cause and Effect

2. Analysing essay titles

Analyse – Break down into the various parts and their relationships
Assess/Evaluate – Decide the worth or value of a subject
Describe – Give a detailed account of something
Discuss – Look at various aspects of a topic, compare benefits and drawbacks
Examine/Explore – Divide into sections and discuss each critically
Illustrate – Give examples
Outline/Trace – Explain a topic briefly and clearly
Suggest – Make a proposal and support it
Summarise – Deal with a complex topic by reducing it to the main elements

(NB: 'summarise' and 'outline' are similar)

3. Practice A

a) Summarise/discuss
Give the factors behind the development, and explore the possible consequences.

b) Describe
List the most likely causes of this situation.

c) What/Are there
Give the advantages and disadvantages.

d) What/Evaluate
List the most important sources, and say how useful they are in reducing CO_2 emissions.

4. Brainstorming

Possible benefits

Young children more open, less inhibited so learn faster

They appear to have better memories

May improve understanding of their own language

Possible drawbacks

Young children may not understand the necessary grammar

They may not grasp the cultural context of a second language

5. Essay length

(NB: These figures are only a guide and individual students may have a different approach)

a) How/Illustrate
Approximately 40:60

b) What are/Are there
Approximately 60:40

c) What are/Evaluate
Approximately 40:60

6. Outlines/Plans

Lists can help develop a logical structure and make it easier to allocate space, but are rather inflexible.

Mind maps are more flexible as extra items can be added easily.

8. Practice B

(Example answers)

b) Higher rates of literacy often lead to greater demand for secondary education.

c) Due to last year's national election, a new government was formed.

d) Installing speed cameras on main roads produced a fall in the number of fatal accidents.

e) Opening a new hospital reduced infant mortality.

f) More people shopping on the internet results in stores closing on the high street.

9. Practice C

(Other answers possible)

a) because of/due to/owing to

b) because/since/as

c)   consequently/therefore/which is why/hence
d)   due to/owing to/because of
e)   because of/due to/owing to
f)   so/therefore/thus/consequently

10. Progress check

a)   *(Example paragraph)*

An increase of 25% in the price of oil would have various likely results. First, it might lead to sharp rises in the cost of transport and freight, thus affecting the price of most goods. Clearly, businesses for which fuel was a significant proportion of their costs, such as airlines, would find it difficult to maintain profitability. Another consequence would be a reduction in oil consumption as marginal users switched to alternative fuels, such as gas, or made economies. There would also be increased investment in exploration for oil, as the oil companies attempted to increase supply, and this in turn would stimulate demand for equipment such as oil rigs. Finally, there would be a number of more localised effects, for instance a change in demand from larger to smaller and more economical vehicles.

Unit 1.6: Finding Key Points and Note-Making/Using Abbreviations

1.   Why make notes?

(Possible answers)

To avoid plagiarism
To keep a record of reading/lectures
To revise for exams
To help remember main points

2.   Note-making methods

The notes are paraphrased, not copied from the text. The source is included.

4.   Finding relevant points

Key points:

2.   The rate of increase appears to have virtually stopped . . . This trend may have important consequences for the healthcare system: according to a recent study (Finkelstein *et al.*, 2009) an obese American is likely to cost the system over 40% more than someone with normal weight.

3.   . . . but medical researchers still struggle to understand the basic causes of the problem, which is that obesity in America is now three times greater than fifty years ago.

4.   . . . obesity is linked to social class: those with irregular and badly paid employment are more likely to eat what is convenient and tasty . . . Another possibility is that food is now cheaper relative to income . . . people use fewer calories doing domestic chores . . .

5. Practice A

(Example notes)

Source: (Herapath, T. (2012) *Journal of Transatlantic Contexts* 14, p. 319)

<u>Have Americans stopped getting fatter?</u>

1) US govt. efforts to encourage healthy eating may be succeeding
2) Rate of increase in obesity has stalled – may reduce future healthcare costs – obesity adds 40% to medical expenses (Finkelstein *et al.*, 2009)
3) No agreement on reasons for 3x rise obesity in US since 1960s
4) 3 possible causes (related to class):
    a) more people have disorganised lives
    b) food has become cheaper
    c) people do less physical work

9. Practice B

a) information and communications technology/higher education/and others
b) genetically modified/for example
c) Note/curricula vitae/Human Resource Management
d) approximately/before common era
e) Doctor of Philosophy (thesis)/tuberculosis/south east
f) Figure 4/world wide web
g) Vice-Chancellor/Postgraduate Certificate of Education
h) Professor/as soon as possible

10. Progress check

(Example notes)

Source: (Kitschelt, P. (2006) *How the Brain Works*. Berlin: Freihaus, p. 73)

<u>The brain and the memory process</u>

1) Siesta can help improve memory and learning
2) New memories > hippocampus (short term) > Pre-frontal cortex (long-term)
3) Process happens during Stage 2 sleep
4) Univ. Calif. team researched process:
    • 2 groups: a) stayed awake
                   b) had siesta
    • group b performed better at memory tasks in evening

Unit 1.7: Summarising and Paraphrasing/Finding Synonyms

1. Successful summarising

A good summary requires:
selection of most important aspects/clear description/accuracy
1.c > 2.d > 3.b > 4.a > 5.e

2. Practice A

1 = a (contains all key points)
2 = b (includes information not in original e.g. increase in profits, and fails to mention some points)

3. Practice B

b) *(Example answers – includes answers for a)*
   i)   Falling levels of fertility have generally been found as countries become richer.
   ii) In some, number of children born has fallen below replacement rate.
   iii) Two results: smaller populations and larger numbers of elderly needing support.
   iv) Recent research claims that this situation may be changing.
   v)   In most advanced countries, fertility is now rising.

c) *(Example summary)*

The growing family?
Falling levels of fertility have generally been found as countries become richer. In some, the number of children born has fallen below the replacement rate. There are two likely results of this trend: smaller populations and larger numbers of elderly needing support. But recent research claims that this pattern may be changing: it suggests that in most advanced countries, fertility is now rising.

d) *(Example summary)*
Research suggests that the long-term decline in human fertility may be reversing in some of the most advanced societies.

4. Practice C

(Example summary)

The Washlet is an expensive lavatory with a range of special features which is popular in its home market, Japan. Its maker, the Toto company, is hoping to expand sales in the West, but different regulations about toilet design and electrical fittings make this a challenging goal.

6. **Practice D**

1b The best paraphrase, with all main points included and a significantly different structure.

2a Quite good, but lack of precision (at that time) and unsuitable register (bosses).

3c A poor paraphrase, with only a few words changed and extra and inaccurate information added (Britain was the only country . . .).

8. **Practice E**

(A number of possibilities are acceptable here. These are suggestions)

a) It is generally considered that males and females think and behave in different ways. Women seem to have superior memories, better social abilities and are more successful at multi-tasking. Men, by comparison, seem to focus better on subjects and have superior motor and spatial abilities, although obviously many people do not follow these patterns.

b) The explanation for these differences may be the way people behaved thousands of years ago, when men were hunters while women stayed at home as carers for their children. But another approach is to see the behaviour as resulting from the way our brains function.

c) The brain functioning of 428 men and 521 women has been compared using brain scans in recent research by Ragini Verma's team at Pennsylvania University. Fascinating differences were found by tracking the pathways of water molecules around the brain area.

d) The cerebrum is the name for the upper part of the brain, and this consists of left and right halves. It is believed that logic is controlled from the left half, while the right side deals with intuition. Dr Verma's research discovered that the female molecule pathways were mainly between the two parts, but the male pathways were generally within the halves. Her conclusion is that these findings are an explanation for differences in skills between the sexes, for example greater social ability in women in contrast to stronger male focus on single issues.

9. **How synonyms work**

Word/phrase	Synonym
oil	hydrocarbon
company	firm
in the world	global/internationally
people	employees

10. Common synonyms in academic writing

(NB: Some of these pairs are approximate synonyms)

Nouns		Verbs	
area	field	alter	change
authority	source	accelerate	speed up
behaviour	conduct	achieve	reach
beliefs	ethics	analyse	take apart
benefit	advantage	assist	help
category	type	attach	join
component	part	challenge	question
concept	idea	claim	suggest
controversy	argument	clarify	explain
drawback	disadvantage	concentrate on	focus on
expansion	increase	confine	limit
feeling	emotion	develop	evolve
framework	structure	eliminate	remove
goal	target	evaluate	examine
hypothesis	theory	found	establish
interpretation	explanation	maintain	insist
issue	topic	predict	forecast
method	system	prohibit	ban
option	possibility	quote	cite
quotation	citation	raise	increase
results	findings	reduce	decrease
statistics	figures	respond	reply
study	research	retain	keep
trend	tendency	show	demonstrate
output	production	strengthen	reinforce

11. Practice F

(Others are possible)

a) Professor Hicks <u>challenged</u> the <u>results</u> of the <u>study</u>.

b) The <u>figures demonstrate</u> a steady <u>rise</u> in applications.

c) The institute's <u>forecast</u> has caused a major <u>debate</u>.

d) Cost seems to be the <u>principal disadvantage</u> to that <u>method</u>.

e) They will <u>focus on</u> the first <u>possibility</u>.

f) The <u>structure</u> can be <u>kept</u> but the <u>target</u> needs to be <u>modified</u>.

g) OPEC, the oil producers' cartel, is to <u>reduce output</u> to <u>increase</u> global prices.

h) The <u>tendency</u> to smaller families has <u>accelerated</u> in the last decade.

12. Progress check

(Example answer)

Archaeologists can learn about many aspects of historic societies by studying shipwrecks, but most of the millions lying on the ocean floor are too deep for divers to examine. They can only work above 50 metres depth; restricting them to coastal wrecks which are more likely to have been disturbed. Research in mid-ocean has required expensive submarines with their support vessels, limiting the number of wrecks that can be explored. But this may change due to the latest craft, called an automatic underwater vehicle or AUV. Not requiring a support ship and operating independently, this will be used by an American team to examine part of the sea bed off the Egyptian coast close to the site of an ancient harbour.

Unit 1.8: References and Quotations/Using Verbs of Reference

1. Why give references?

<u>Smith (2009)</u> argues that the popularity of the Sports Utility Vehicle (SUV) is irrational, as despite their high cost most are never driven off-road. In his view 'they are bad for road safety, the environment and road congestion' <u>(Smith, 2009:37)</u>.

The first is a summary, the second a quotation.

A summary allows the writer to condense ideas, while a quotation uses the words of the original author, which have authenticity and may be difficult to improve.

4. Practice A

(Example answers)

a) According to Hoffman (2012) mobile phones have had a powerful impact in the developing world as they offer previously unavailable services, and have led to the growth of new, focused local operators.

b) Hoffman points out that the special conditions in the developing world have produced new phone operators: 'that are larger and more flexible than Western companies, and which have grown by catering for poorer customers . . .' (Hoffman 2012:87).

c) Hoffman (2012) argues that the impact of mobile telephony on developing countries is significant as they offer services previously unavailable, and has led to the growth of new local operators which: 'are larger and more flexible than Western companies, and which have grown by catering for poorer customers . . .' (Hoffman 2012:87).

6. Organising the list of references

a)
   i)   Dörnyei
   ii) Bialystock/Larson-Hall
   iii) Flege
   iv) Myles
   v)   The International Commission on Second Language Acquisition
   vi) Gass and Selinker

b) For book and journal titles

c) For titles of books and journals (not articles)

d) Under the name of the organisation or title of the publication

e)
   i)   Bialystock, 1997
   ii)   Dörnyei, 2009
   iii) Flege, 1999
   iv)   Gass and Selinker, 2001
   v)   Larson-Hall, 2008
   vi)   Myles, nd
   vii) The International Commission on Second Language Acquisition, nd

7. Reference verbs

(Some other verbs may be possible)

a) A admitted/accepted that he might have made a mistake . . .

b) B denied saying that women make/made better doctors than men.

c) C stated/claimed/argued that small firms are/were more dynamic than large ones.

d) D agreed with C's views on small firms.

e) E assumed/presumed that most people work for money.

f) F concluded that allergies are/were becoming more common.

g) G doubted that electric cars will/would replace conventional ones.

h) H hypothesised/suggested a link between crime and sunspot activity.

8. Further referring verbs

(Other verbs may be possible)

a) L criticised/censured her research methods.

b) M identified/classified four main types of children in care.

c) N commended the company for its record for workplace safety.

d) O interpreted the noises whales make/made as expressions of happiness.

e) P identified/presented wind power and biomass as the leading green energy sources in the future.

f) Q described/portrayed Darwin as the most influential naturalist of the nineteenth century.

9. Progress check

Although tool-making ability had been thought unique to primates, recent research by an Oxford University team has demonstrated that crows can also develop tools (Grummitt, 2010). The birds had previously been observed in the wild using sticks to reach food, but the Oxford team gave crows lengths of wire which the birds bent to extract chunks of meat from inside a glass tube. As Grummitt explains: 'the Oxford experiment was designed to see if the same kind of bird could modify this ability to make a tool out of a material not found in their native forests i.e. wire.' (Grummitt 2010:15)

Grummitt, F. (2010) *What Makes Us Human?* Dublin: Roseberry Press

Unit 1.9: Combining Sources/Providing Cohesion

1. Mentioning sources

a) 6

b) The level of technology anxiety

c) Venkatesh

d) Mick and Fournier

e) 2

2. Taking a critical approach

a) *(Example answers)*

. . . steps should be taken to reduce future warming by restricting the output of greenhouse gases such as carbon dioxide.	. . . it can be expected that . . . burning of fossil fuels.
She mentions evidence of historical climate change which cannot have been caused by rising levels of CO_2 . . .	Some critics claim . . . unrelated to CO_2 levels.

b) puts forward/maintains/presents/mentions/discusses/considers

c) However

d) But/on the other hand

3. **Practice A**

   (Example answer)

   There is good evidence that globalisation has resulted in a considerable increase in world trade over the past 20–30 years (Costa, 2008). However, it has been pointed out that the benefits of this are not evenly shared. While multi-nationals are able to use the cheapest labour for manufacturing, people in the poorest countries are no better off than they were 40 years ago (Lin, 2006). In addition, these large companies benefit from reduced import duties and so can compete more successfully with local businesses, further strengthening their market dominance (Brokaw, 2012).

5. **Practice B**

Reference	References word/phrase
La Ferrera	She
new businesses	they
average life of only 4.7 years	this
one economic	the former
one social	the latter
the former . . ., the latter	these

7. **Practice C**

   Velcro is a fabric fastener used with clothes and shoes. **It** was invented by a Swiss engineer called George de Mestral. **His** idea was derived from studying the tiny hooks found on some plant seeds. **They** cling to animals and help disperse the seeds. Velcro has two sides, one of which is covered in small hooks and the other in loops. When **they** are pressed together they form a strong bond.

   Mestral spent eight years perfecting **his** invention, which **he** called 'Velcro' from the French words 'velour' and 'crochet'. **It** was patented in 1955 and today over 60 million metres of Velcro are sold annually.

8. **Progress check**

   (Example answer)

   Wallace Carothers, the director of research at the American DuPont Corporation, invented nylon in 1935. He had previously studied chemistry, and specialised in polymers, which are molecules composed of long chains of atoms. Nylon was a strong but fine synthetic fibre which was first mass produced in 1939. It was/is used to make a wide range of products which included/include stockings, toothbrushes, parachutes, fishing lines, and surgical thread.

Unit 1.10: Organising Paragraphs/Using Conjunctions

1. **Paragraph structure**

The answers are found below the table.

2. **Practice A**

a) Topic sentence
Example
Reason
Supporting point 1
Supporting point 2
Supporting point 3

b) for instance/It is widely believed/In addition/But above all

c) Despite this

3. **Development of ideas**

a) | Topic sentence | iv |
    | --- | --- |
    | Definition | ii |
    | Result 1 | i |
    | Result 2 | vi |
    | Result 3 | v |
    | Conclusion | iii |

b) All these claims

c) These/but/When this/Others/in other words/Even

5. **Practice B**

(Example answer)

Bill Gates was born in 1955, the second child in a middle-class Seattle family. At the age of 13 he became interested in writing computer programmes, and in 1975 Gates and his school friend Allen started a programming business called Microsoft. In 1980 IBM asked their company to write an operating system for IBM's new PC. This system was called MS-DOS. Five years later Microsoft launched the Windows operating system, and by 1995 Gates was the richest man in the world. He stepped down from working at Microsoft in 2006 to focus on running his charitable foundation.

6. **Types of conjunctions**

    a) A few inventions, <u>for instance</u> television, have had a major impact on everyday life.

    b) <u>Furthermore</u>, many patients were treated in clinics and surgeries.

    c) The definition of 'special needs' is important <u>since</u> it is the cause of some disagreement.

    d) The technology allows consumers a choice, <u>thus</u> increasing their sense of satisfaction.

    e) Four hundred people were interviewed for the survey, <u>then</u> the results were analysed.

    f) <u>However</u>, another body of opinion associates globalisation with unfavourable outcomes.

        ii) Result   (d)

        iii) Reason   (c)

        iv) Opposition (f)

        v) Example   (a)

        vi) Time   (e)

7. **Practice C**

Conjunction	Type		Conjunction	Type
a) such as	example	f)	In other words	example
b) but	opposition	g)	instead of	opposition
c) Although	opposition	h)	Consequently	result
d) for instance	example	i)	and	addition
e) however	opposition	j)	neither . . . nor	opposition

8. **Common conjunctions**

(Others are possible)

Addition: moreover/as well as/in addition/and/also/furthermore/plus

Result: therefore/consequently/so/that is why (see Unit 1.5)

Reason: because/owing to/as a result of/as/since/due to (see Unit 1.5)

Opposition: but/yet/while/however/nevertheless/whereas/albeit/although/despite

Example: such as/e.g./in particular/for instance (see Unit 1.4)

Time: after/while/then/next/subsequently

9. **Practice D**

(Others are possible)

a) After
b) Although/While
c) moreover/furthermore/additionally
d) therefore/so
e) for instance/for example
f) Due to/Because of
g) While
h) As/Because/Since

10. Conjunctions of opposition

(Example answers)

a) i) Although the government claimed that inflation was falling, the opposition said it was rising.

   ii) The government claimed that inflation was falling while the opposition said it was rising.

b) i) This department must reduce expenditure, yet it needs to install new computers.

   ii) While this department must reduce expenditure it also needs to install new computers.

11. Progress check

(Example answer)

Trams were first introduced in the late nineteenth century, when they provided cheap and convenient mass transport in many cities in America and Europe. But their drawbacks were that the rail-based systems were expensive to maintain, and the fixed tracks made them inflexible as cities developed. Consequently, by the 1950s many European and Asian cities had closed their tramway systems.

However, today trams are re-gaining their popularity. They are seen as less polluting than cars and relatively cheap to operate. As a result, cities such as Paris and Manchester have built new systems. Yet the high cost of constructing tramways and difficulties with traffic congestion blocking the tracks mean that trams remain a controversial transport option.

Unit 1.11: Introductions and Conclusions/Giving Definitions

1. Introduction contents

a) **Components**   **Y/N**

   i)   A definition of any unfamiliar terms in the title   Y
   ii)   Your opinions on the subject of the essay   N
   iii) An outline of the main body of the essay   Y
   iv) A provocative idea or question to interest the reader   N
   v)   Your aim or purpose in writing   Y
   vi) The method you adopt to answer the question   Y
   vii) Some brief background to the topic   Y
   viii) Any limitations you set yourself   Y
   ix) Mention of some sources you have read on the topic   Y

The order of components is discussed in section 2

b)   A) Background
      B) Outline
      C) Purpose
      D) Mention of sources
      E) Definition
      F) Limitation

3 Opening sentences

(Example answers)

a)   In the past decade global warming or climate change has become one of the most pressing issues on the international agenda.

b)   There has been some decline in rates of infant mortality in the developing world over the last twenty years, but in many countries progress has been slow.

c)   Significant internal migration from the countryside to the cities is a feature of many developing societies.

4 Conclusions

   a) Y
   b) Y
   c) N
   d) Y
   e) Y

f) Y

g) Y

h) N

i) f

ii) b

iii) e

iv) d

v) g

vi) a

5. Practice A

1 (v)

2 (iii)

3 (i)

4 (iv)

5 (ii)

6. Simple definitions

a) instrument

b) organs

c) organisation

d) material

e) behaviour

f) process

g) period

h) grains

(Example answers)

i) A lecture is an academic talk used for teaching purposes.

j) An idiom is a phrase used in colloquial language.

7. Complex definitions

a) a failed project

b) development

c) attachment

d) globalisation

i) c

ii) a

iii) b, d

8. **Progress check**

(Example definitions)

a) **Capital punishment** involves the execution by the state of convicted criminals.

b) An **entrepreneurial business** is set up by somebody who demonstrates the effective application of a number of enterprising attributes, such as creativity, initiative, risk-taking, problem-solving ability and autonomy, and will often risk his or her own capital.

c) **E-books** are books in digital form which can be read on electronic devices.

d) **Urban areas** are predominantly built-up areas in which roads, housing or commercial buildings are found.

e) **Obesity** is a medical term meaning unhealthily overweight.

Unit 1.12: Rewriting and Proofreading/Academic Style

2. **Practice A**

(Example rewrite)

Organisations inevitably face risks by permitting researchers to interview employees, so these must be understood and minimised by the design of the research project. If employees criticise other workers in the organisation they may be punished, or alternatively they may feel unable to express their true feelings and so invalidate the interviews. Consequently, researchers must protect the reputation of the organisation and the value of their own work by carefully explaining the purpose of the study and insisting on strict anonymity through the use of false names. By doing this both parties should benefit from the research.

3. **Proofreading**

i) Africa is not a country: *such as Nigeria*

ii) Innocence is a noun: *Young and innocent*

iii) Question mark needed

iv) Present perfect needed with 'since': *Since 2005 there have been . . .*

v) 'Successfulness' is not a word: *success*

vi) 'pervious' is incorrect: *previous*

vii) 'one of the . . .' needs plural noun: *one of the largest companies . . .*

viii) repetition: the essay will conclude with an analysis of . . .

ix) time periods need definite article: *the nineteenth century*

x) *when consumers go out shopping . . .*

4. **Practice B**

(Corrected version)

The/a bicycle is one of the most efficient machines ever designed. Cyclists can travel four times faster than walkers, while using less energy to do so. Various people invented early versions of the bike, but the first model with pedals which was successfully mass-produced was made by a Frenchman, Ernest Michaux, in 1861. Later additions included pneumatic tyres and gears. Today hundreds of millions of bicycles are in use all over the world.

7. **Practice C**

(Example sentences)

a) Another factor to consider is the possibility of crime increasing.
b) Currently the rate of unemployment is high.
c) In the near future a vaccine for malaria may be discovered.
d) After 1989 the value of Japanese property fell sharply.
e) The numbers in that report are unreliable.
f) The severe inflation led to poverty and social unrest.
g) He was delighted to win the prize.
h) Students should be paid to study.
i) Women were enfranchised in 1987.
j) The main causes of the Russian revolution were war and misgovernment.

8. **Varying sentence length**

(Example answer)

Worldwide, enrolments in higher education are increasing. In developed countries over half of all young people enter college, while similar trends are seen in China and South America. This growth has put financial strain on state university systems, so that many countries are asking students and parents to contribute financially. This leads to a debate about whether students or society benefit from tertiary education.

9. **The use of caution**

(Others are possible)

Modals: might/may/could/should
Adverbs: often/usually/frequently/generally/commonly/mainly/apparently
Verb/phrase: seems to/appears to/in general/by and large/it appears/it seems

10. Using modifiers

a) The company's efforts to save energy were quite/fairly successful.

b) The survey was (a fairly/quite a) comprehensive study of student opinion.

c) His second book had a rather hostile reception.

d) The first year students were quite fascinated by her lectures.

e) The latest type of arthritis drug is rather expensive.

11. Progress check

(Example answer)

Despite the growing demand for energy world-wide there is considerable debate about the most appropriate sources. Although coal is inexpensive it is very polluting, while burning gas also produces CO_2. This is not the case with nuclear power, which is often seen as a solution, but this technology is expensive and potentially dangerous. Renewable sources such as wind and solar power do not contribute to global warming but are limited by weather variables. Clearly, there is no simple solution to this question.

Part 2: Elements of Writing

Unit 2.1: Academic Vocabulary: Nouns and Adjectives

2. Nouns

(NB: Not all these words have close synonyms. This list is a guide to approximate meaning. Students should use a dictionary for a full understanding.)

accuracy – precision

analysis – examination

approach – angle of study

assessment – test

assumption – informed guess

authority – expert

category – type

claim – argument

controversy – debate

correlation – link

deterrent – disincentive

emphasis – weight put on one area

evidence – proof

exception – different thing

extract – part of a longer work

ideology – belief
implication – unstated suggestion
innovation – new introduction
intuition – understanding without thinking
motivation – incentive
perspective – angle of study
phenomenon – unusual event
policy – formal guidelines
preference – favourite choice
process – series of stages
proposal – suggestion
provision – supply
sequence – series of stages
strategy – plan
substitute – replacement
technique – method
validity – truth

a)   evidence
b)   suggestions
c)   intuition
d)   provision
e)   claim

3.   Using nouns and adjectives

Noun	Adjective	Noun	Adjective
approximation	approximate	particularly	particular
superiority	superior	reason	reasonable
strategy	strategic	synthesis	synthetic
politics	political	economic/economy	economic/al
industry	industrial	culture	cultural
exterior	external	average	average
height	high	reliability	reliable
heat	hot	strength	strong
confidence	confident	truth	true
width	wide	probability	probable
necessity	necessary	length	long
danger	dangerous	relevance	relevant

4. **Practice A**

   a) confident
   b) particularities/strengths
   c) probability
   d) relevant
   e) necessary
   f) danger
   g) necessity
   h) approximate
   i) economic
   j) synthesis

5. **Academic adjectives**

   absolute (not common as noun)
   abstract
   accuracy
   ambiguity
   analysis
   effectiveness
   exclusivity
   logic
   metaphor
   precision
   reason
   reliability
   relevance
   specificity
   subjectivity
   theory

6. **Practice B**

   a) strategic – strategy
   b) analytical – analysis
   c) synthetic – synthesis
   d) major – majority
   e) cultural – culture
   f) theoretical – theory
   g) frequent – frequency
   h) critical – criticism/critic
   i) Social – society
   j) practical – practice

Unit 2.2: Academic Vocabulary: Verbs and Adverbs

1. Understanding main verbs

(Approximate synonyms)

adapt – modify
arise – occur
conduct – carry out
characterise – have features of
clarify – explain
concentrate on – look at closely
be concerned with – deal with
demonstrate – show
determine – find
discriminate – distinguish
establish – found
exhibit – show
focus on – look at closely
generate – create
hold – be true
identify – pick out
imply – suggest
interact – work together
interpret – explain
manifest – show
overcome – defeat
propose – suggest
prove – turn out
recognise – accept
relate to – link to
supplement – add to
undergo – experience
yield – produce

2. Practice A

(Some other verbs may be possible)

a) proposed
b) arose
c) clarify
d) adapted
e) focuses on/concentrates on

f)   identified
g)   conducted
h)   demonstrates

4.   Practice B

a)   psychologically
b)   Originally
c)   Alternatively
d)   Recently
e)   Similarly
f)   Traditionally

Unit 2.3: Making Comparisons

3.   Practice A

a)   Real Madrid was the richest club **in European football**.
b)   Real Madrid's income was almost twice **as** much as AC Milan's.
c)   FC Barcelona earned **considerably** more than Manchester City.
d)   Juventus had less revenue **than** Arsenal.
e)   Chelsea's income was **significantly** lower than Bayern Munich's.
f)   Manchester United earned approximately **the** same as Bayern Munich.

4.   Practice B

a)   shows/compares/contrasts
b)   rate
c)   varies/fluctuates
d)   same
e)   slightly
f)   than
g)   over/approximately
h)   high

Unit 2.4: Numbers

2.   Percentages

a)   50%
b)   100%
c)   400%

3. Further numerical phrases

(Example answers)

a) The price of petrol has increased tenfold since 1975.

b) Two thirds of the students in the group were women.

c) The new high-speed train halved the journey time to Madrid.

d) The number of students applying for the Psychology course has risen by 50%.

e) More than twice as many British students as Italian students complete their first degree course.

f) Tap water is seven hundred times cheaper than bottled water.

g) The highest rate of unemployment is in Spain and the lowest in Norway.

h) A majority of members supported the suggestion, but a large proportion of these expressed some doubts.

4. Practice A

(Example answers)

b) There were twice as many sports at the Paris Olympics compared to the Athens games.

c) The number of athletes competing doubled between the Tokyo and Beijing Olympics.

d) In the Barcelona Olympics nearly a third of the athletes were women.

e) The number of Olympic sports rose threefold between 1896 and 2008.

f) The number of events has risen steadily over the last century.

g) A substantial minority of athletes at the Beijing Olympics were women.

5. Practice B

(Model paragraph)

The 15 students in the group spoke six different languages, but a small majority spoke Chinese. Management was the future course for nearly half, with Economics for one fifth of the students, while Finance and MBA each attracted two students. Only one of the group was over 23, and their favourite sports were swimming, followed by football, dancing and climbing.

Unit 2.5: Passives

2. Structure

a) The data was collected and the two groups (were) compared.
b) 120 people in three social classes were interviewed.
c) The results were checked and several errors (were) found.
d) An analysis of the findings will be made.
e) Four doctors were asked to give their opinions.
f) The report was written and ten copies (were) distributed.

3. Using adverbs

a) The company was profitably run by the Connors family until 1981.
b) It has been optimistically predicted that prisons will be unnecessary in the future (by Dr Weber).
c) All students in the exam were helpfully provided with pencils.
d) The percentages were accurately calculated to three decimal places (by researchers).
e) The essays were punctually handed in on Tuesday morning.

4. Practice

Passive	Active possible?	Active
He was worn out	Yes	The effort . . . had worn him out
He was born	No	
John was concerned by	Yes	The situation of the poor concerned John . . .
a (. . .) shop which was called	Yes	which he called . . .
John was helped financially	Yes	his father-in-law helped him . . .
the business was taken over	Yes	his wife took the business over . . .
she was soon assisted	Yes	their 10-year-old son assisted her
He had been created Baron Trent	No	

The effect of using the passive throughout would be to make the tone very formal.

Unit 2.6: Prepositions

1. Types of prepositions

Noun + preposition	reasons for/growth of/development of/expansion of
Verb + preposition	made by
Adjective + preposition	relevant to
Phrasal verb	sets out
Preposition of place	in Asia
Preposition of time	in the twentieth century
Phrase	in particular/in detail

2. Practice A

b) adjective + preposition
c) verb + preposition
d) preposition of place
e) noun + preposition
f) phrase

3. Prepositions and nouns

a) of
b) in
c) of
d) to
e) in/on

4. Prepositions in phrases

a) on
b) of
c) of
d) in
e) of
f) on
g) in
h) of

5. Prepositions of place and time

a)   Among
b)   from, to/between, and
c)   in, of
d)   in, in
e)   in, at
f)   On, between
g)   around, of/on

7. Practice B

a)   focused on/concentrated on
b)   pointed out
c)   associated with
d)   divided into
e)   blamed for
f)   believed in

Unit 2.7: Punctuation

9. Practice A

a)   The study was carried out by Christine Zhen-Wei Qiang of the National University of Singapore.
b)   Professor Rowan's new book 'The End of Privacy' (2014) is published in New York.

or

Professor Rowan's new book *The End of Privacy* (2014) is published in New York.
c)   As Keynes said: 'It's better to be roughly right than precisely wrong'.
d)   Three departments, Law, Business and Economics, have had their funding cut.
e)   Thousands of new words such as 'app' enter the English language each year.
f)   The BBC's World Service is broadcast in 33 languages including Somali and Vietnamese.
g)   She scored 56% on the main course; the previous semester she had achieved 67%.

10. Practice B

The School of Biomedical Sciences at Borchester University is offering two undergraduate degree courses in Neuroscience this year. Students can study either Neuroscience with Pharmacology or Neuroscience with Biochemistry. There is also a Master's course which runs for four years and involves a period of study abroad during November and December. Professor Andreas Fischer is course leader for Neuroscience and enquiries should be sent to him via the website.

Unit 2.8: Singular or Plural?

1. **Five areas of difficulty**
   a) . . . and disadvantages   (e)
   b) are vaccinated   (a)
   c) rural areas   (c)
   d) . . . in crime   (b)
   e) Each company has its own policy (d)

4. **Practice A**
   a) Little
   b) businesses
   c) experience/is
   d) travel broadens
   e) much advice
   f) few interests
   g) civil war
   h) work

5. **Practice B**

   companies have/websites/e-commerce/this is/businesses/companies/their/trouble/security/expense/mean/these companies

Unit 2.9: Time Markers

3. **Practice A**
   a) Recently
   b) until
   c) for
   d) Last month
   e) by
   f) Since

4. **Practice B**
   a) Last
   b) During/On
   c) By

d) for
e) ago
f) later
g) until
h) Currently/Now

5. Practice C

(Example answer)

Napoleon entered military school in 1784 at the age of 15, five years before the French revolution began. In 1793 he was promoted to brigadier-general, and when only 27 he became commander of the army in Italy, and also married Josephine. On his return from Egypt in 1799 he became the First Consul of France, and by 1807 France was in control of most of Europe. Three years later he divorced Josephine and married Marie-Louise, the Austrian emperor's daughter. But in 1812 Napoleon and his army were forced to retreat from Russia, and in 1814 he was exiled to Elba. After his defeat at the battle of Waterloo a year later he was again exiled, to St Helena, where he lived until his death in 1821.

Unit 2.10 Visual Information

1. Types of visuals

Types	Uses	Example
1 diagram	d	F
2 table	f	B
3 map	a	G
4 pie chart	c	D
5 flow chart	g	E
6 bar chart	b	C
7 line graph	e	A

2. The language of change

a) rose/increased
b) levelled off
c) climbed/increased/rose
d) steadily

e) slightly
f) rose/climbed/increased
g) peak
h) fell/decreased/dropped/decline
i) sharply/steeply

3. Describing visuals

i) is better. It comments on the main features of the chart but does not repeat the statistics.

5. Practice A

a) shows/illustrates
b) various/certain
c) between
d) majority
e) substantially/significantly
f) Spain
g) than

6. Practice B

(Example paragraph)

The table illustrates student evaluation of library facilities, contrasting under-graduate with graduate opinion. Most facilities are rated highly by both groups, especially the café and staff helpfulness. Both student groups are least satisfied with the availability of short loan stock. In most areas graduates seem slightly more critical of facilities than undergraduates.

Part 3: Writing Models

Unit 3.1: Reports

2. Essays and reports

1) Essay
2) Report
3) Report
4) Report
5) Essay

3. Survey report

a) conducted
b) random
c) questionnaire
d) questioned
e) respondents/interviewees
f) Interviewees/Respondents
g) mentioned
h) majority
i) slightly
j) minority
k) questions
l) common
m) generally
n) sample

4. Practice

Introduction

a) Due to the recent closure of the maintenance depot, a site approximately 250 metres long and 100 metres wide has recently become vacant on the west side of the university campus.

b) The aim of the redevelopment is to improve facilities for both staff and students, and at the same time enhance the appearance of this part of the campus.

c) Two alternatives schemes for redevelopment have been put forward, as can be seen in Plans A and B above.

d) This report attempts to compare the two schemes on this basis and to establish which is the more suitable.

e) The report takes into account a consultation exercise with staff and students carried out last autumn.

(Example report)

Proposals

The central feature of plan A is a circular park area in the middle of the site, which would contain trees and seating. On one side of this is a small car park, with space for twenty vehicles. On the other side is a block of tennis courts. The alternative, plan B, provides a larger car park along the side next to the Access Road, with spaces for 50 cars. The other half of the site contains a building housing a café and a range of shops at one end, while at the other end is a swimming pool.

<u>Discussion</u>

Clearly the two proposals offer quite different amenities. Plan A provides some green space for relaxation, along with tennis courts and a limited amount of parking. It is a relatively low-key scheme that could be completed quite cheaply. In contrast, Plan B would be more expensive, but would also offer catering and sporting facilities as well as extra parking.

<u>Recommendations</u>

It can be argued in favour of plan B that a swimming pool would have wider appeal than tennis courts, and also that there is a severe shortage of parking on the campus. However, it is not clear that more shops and a café are really needed for the university, and few students actually drive cars. Plan A would also do more to improve the look of the campus by increasing the green space. In view of these considerations the university should perhaps consider combining the best of both plans, and replace the tennis courts in Plan A with a swimming pool.

Unit 3.2: Longer Essays

2. Example essay

a) The writer appears to be in favour of nuclear energy.

b) The writer presents the arguments against nuclear power and attempts to show their weakness. In the conclusion the writer summarises his/her position ('nuclear energy can be seen . . . fossil fuels').

3. Revision

(Example answers)

a) See Paragraph 1.

b) 'This essay attempts to assess the risks of using nuclear power, in comparison with other sources of energy'.

c) 'The main arguments for employing nuclear energy are first considered, followed by an examination of the safety issues around this source of power, including the safety and security concerns connected with nuclear waste'.

d) '. . .alternative energy sources to fossil fuels i.e. oil, gas and coal . . .'

e) 'Wind energy and solar power are frequently presented as alternative energy sources to fossil fuels'.

f) 'Mtoe (million tons of oil equivalent)'

g) '. . .since the Chernobyl accident in 1986 there has been persistent concern . . .'

h) 'As a result, the demand for total primary energy, which will accompany the population growth, is projected to increase . . .'

i) power
j) 'If this increase occurs the total global stock of oil and gas would only be adequate for 250 years . . .'
k) 'It is estimated that in 2003, in the USA, nuclear energy prevented the release of 680 million tons of CO_2 . . .'
l) 'However, its opponents argue that it can damage the environment by creating radioactive waste'.
m) Bodansky (2004)
n) 'Lillington (2004) suggests that the cost of purchasing fuel for nuclear energy is likely to remain low compared to other energy sources . . .'

Test Your Progress

Writing an essay

(Other answers may be possible)

a) stage/part/step
b) the/its
c) for
d) Second/Then
e) and
f) critically/rigorously/carefully
g) which
h) skills/techniques
i) answer
j) be
k) taking
l) you
m) checking/ensuring
n) After
o) maximum
p) to
q) tables/graphs/figures
r) should/must

Index